Seven Stages of Grief, When You Leave the Police

About the Author

I prefer the stories of others.

Dear Nicky ✶

Can't wait to read or hear all your stories ♡

Best wishes and thankyou
Charlotte for the gold
standard ☺

Charlotte Gearing

Seven Stages of Grief, When You Leave the Police

Olympia Publishers
London

www.olympiapublishers.com
OLYMPIA PAPERBACK EDITION

Copyright © Charlotte Gearing 2023

The right of Charlotte Gearing to be identified as author of
this work has been asserted in accordance with sections 77 and 78 of
the Copyright, Designs and Patents Act 1988.

All Rights Reserved

No reproduction, copy or transmission of this publication
may be made without written permission.
No paragraph of this publication may be reproduced,
copied or transmitted save with the written permission of the publisher,
or in accordance with the provisions
of the Copyright Act 1956 (as amended).

Any person who commits any unauthorised act in relation to
this publication may be liable to criminal
prosecution and civil claims for damage.

A CIP catalogue record for this title is
available from the British Library.

ISBN: 978-1-80439-099-3

This is a work of creative nonfiction. The events are portrayed to the
best of the author's memory. While all the stories in this book are true,
some names and identifying details have been changed to protect the
privacy of the people involved.

First Published in 2023

Olympia Publishers
Tallis House
2 Tallis Street
London
EC4Y 0AB

Printed in Great Britain

Dedication

To the few beleaguered colleagues, friends, and family, who were unconditionally there and got to know me outside of work. To my family, the Community, Occupational Health, the NHS, GP at hand and Harley Therapy platform – still here.

Acknowledgements

I tried, I did what we're supposed to do.

Contents

Intro 13
Chapter 1 Bargaining 22
Chapter 2 Guilt 42
Chapter 3 Denial 52
Chapter 4 Anger 69
Chapter 5 Sadness 74
Chapter 6 Depression 80
Chapter 7 Acceptance 83
Chapter 8 The Last Job 96
Finale 120

Intro

Who is this absolute nobody writing here? Just who do they think they are? Why does the experience of this girl, woman, other, matter? I was asked to define my own perception of my gender once, and I likened it to an 'it', consisting of oscillating neurons. "I exist", I said.

The girl, woman, other, 'it' – me – was that first responder to your problem, is who. If they could get there on their foot patrol quick enough.

The absolute stranger entering your premises, trying to sort head from tail. Sometimes you asked me to be there, sometimes you didn't. Sometimes you didn't even know I was there. But I was there.

This is my story. Some of it.

This is my story of how I left a police career I wanted to achieve, a police career I loved – right from work experience and seeing morgue photos of an acquaintance. Right through to resignation, and the new life beyond that came from an existence in police service. Other careers are out there and available. A job can be just a job in the end. An important lesson I learnt since resigning, when introducing myself now, is to say I'm me, I'm *working as* a tube operator. Rather than to say I'm me and I'm a tube operator. I'm me, I used to work in the police, too. An osteopath and great teacher taught me that.

Perhaps you're reading this having done the same. Recently resigned or quit from a job you thought you loved. Maybe you were sacked or retired. Or perhaps you were made redundant. I know a few of these, they will tell their stories by the end of this too. Hopefully, more will tell of their experience also. If it echoes that of mine, they will tell it better. I prefer the stories of others.

Others' stories inspired me along the way. Their stories corrected me when I thought all 'bad' cops should be sacked.

I was wrong about that.

Good cops get sacked too and that is really sad.

There is a register to hold their name on, to make sure they definitely do not get reemployed by another police service again. A register that could be better reserved for the worst offending police officers and staff. Not those caught aimlessly in the crossfire, without ill-will or intention.

What that register now amounts to for some is a career full of hard graft over for good. You can only ever be as good as your last job. And if that job goes *very* badly, becomes a 'cluster-fuck', that is what you will be remembered, dealt, and registered for.

A 'cluster-fuck' is a term used in the police when it all goes a bit 'tits-up' and Wrong with a capital W.

My last job, I will come to – I showed *them* how it could and should be done, that was my sign off to both British Transport Police and the Metropolitan Police. Both jurisdictions also within that of the City of London Police borders.

None of them would attend this last call, as I had requested them to. I wasn't allowed to deal with it either, being stuck on mandatory restrictions by senior managers and warned about following 'lawful' orders by bosses.

It was my ex-husband who stood me down for that last job.

"Come home. If you call the police and no one comes, who

do you call on next," he said.

I think he was more disappointed in them than me.

It is surprising to me that, in the end, I didn't want to get sacked for disobeying orders. Whether they were lawful or not is always up for conjecture. Most of my career this far, it hadn't really fazed me – getting sacked. Before that point where I chose to resign and walk away.

I always knew whatever boundaries I had been pushing within the rank-and-file organisation, I couldn't be sacked because what I was doing was what I believed to be fundamentally right and the best course of action for subject, person, object, or place – and all importantly, organisational reputation. As well as the late Her Majesty (HM) the Queen's peace.

When it goes badly, it isn't the people or offenders involved who get labelled or blamed so much, it's the failings within the police service that do.

"It could have been prevented."

"You should have done your job."

Sentiments I can't agree more with. Reports I read of what small difference in approach could have made, if only that preventative opportunity had been taken by an officer responding to a call for service.

Let's not forget though, that a front-line officer is the leading representative of a whole heap of others behind them in any chain of command. You just can't see them all that much, if at all. Unless it's Monday 8:31a.m and you so happen to be loitering in some grey corridor, you perhaps wish you weren't in.

Perhaps you're reading this at a crossroads point in your life. Or having seen all the media and marketing to 'join the police' are thinking about it. Something worth considering once in the police service, the media whatever you go on to do – bad or good, can often refer to this part of your CV.

I left the career with every intention to be able to 'go back again' on a part-time basis. Technically, at the time of resignation there was no other alternative in me staying part-time, as permission for both careers was not yet granted. I was told you could return within five years. They write to retired cops, asking them to come back. So why not to those who resigned? A sign of one rule for some, another rule for others. What I experienced, now on the outside, was the brick wall of human resources (HR). They wouldn't enter into any dialogue with me once I had left. Not even a Microsoft Teams meeting, or so they said. My 'return' was a safety net to have and to hold, amongst all the sea of uncertainty and change. A change of career will do that to you. Perhaps that was rather naïve of me, thinking I would or could go back.

Could I have left sooner? Probably. But fact be told, I didn't want to. It had to be the right opportunity for me to have to go, to leave, to walk away.

Why? Because in the end I was tired and I had tried to be there for other people. But when the chips went down for me, fairly often, who was really there for me in the end, quite often just me. Or the dog. Or it felt that way sometimes.

No one is going to help you in the end but you. The help you need. It has to come from you.

After I resigned and left, I could have done with someone. or something like this self-help parable, to steady me through when it came to me after the denial stages were over that I had really gone and left the police service. So, here it is. A story of that journey to re-establishing my identity.

Don't get me wrong, I'm not the original creator of all these good ideas – philanthropists and philosophers span a little further along than any of us can go back.

There is no such thing as a good idea that hasn't been thought of already by someone else just like you or just like me.

In the police, we used to call it reinventing the wheel.

They liked doing that and renaming it. Community policing, neighbourhood policing, what about neighbourhood plus?

The community hasn't gone anywhere whilst you've been procrastinating names. It may have changed a bit, but fundamentally it is the glial cells that may be found within the very fabric of a happy enough, all-rounded society.

I think we live in one of them here in the UK, most of the time. Except when anyone implores one not to panic buy, whilst simultaneously topping up for themselves mid-sentence. It all comes to look a bit rather shabby in parts.

Only because those who can, stock up. But what about the rest who can't? I think consider them.

I stepped up to the plate to the office of constable, I'm proud I did – I'm proud I at least tried.

No one is going to pat you on your back and say thank you and well done – I know this now.

It's why I endeavour to say thank you and well done a lot more to others going forward, until I retire my boots next time that is.

I always had a hunch I'd retire in my thirties. I have an entrepreneur instinct.

I sort of have retired. Or feel I have anyway.

Although any official retirement is quite a long way off.

So, here it is. Here is my self-help contribution, some tools

I used to see me through *change*.

For it is massive to be able to say I chose an alternative path to that which was laying or planned in front of me.

Everyone knows the police. Or thinks they know the police.

I chose to do something alternative, to choose another option. Ultimately, I turned to me, to be able to say I can do more than this.

I see my worth.

If no-one is willing to facilitate growth for me within an establishment, then I will facilitate my own change, create my own luck outside of it. The thing is, you have to rely on others to endorse your training or promotion in the police, it is really very hard to achieve progression without it.

Perhaps institution is a better term to use. There is a 'thing' called institutional neurosis. That is where people become institutionalised. It happened in the asylums, before they were closed down. Behaviours which could be observed as apathy, lack of initiative, loss of interest, and submissiveness. Can you see that in any of your colleagues? I failed to become institutionalised, I was deinstitutionalise-able. I wanted to get on and do my job, at the end of the day. With the person in front of me my sole focus. That meant adapting to change. It meant adapting the system to meet their needs if I could.

To leave, I thought it's my life after all, and I would like to look back saying I lived it all as well as I could. Helping others where I could along the way. My view is that you should try to leave people, property and places better than how you found them.

All my achievements and successes have been ethically achieved, not off the sweat, blood, or tears of another human being – all my endeavours are my own, created and embroiled.

Authentic as they come. I take no credit for another's work, where I have not created it my own way and understanding of it. That itself takes toil. We can't possibly know everything we don't know yet. If someone else has said the exact same words as can be found in my story, then well done to them too.

I am culminating together what I think isn't out there, or at least what I couldn't find when I went looking for it. That is a female police officer, all in one place, that has resigned from the police service to try and do something else.

You do see the odd newspaper report of when some female cops have sued for constructive dismissal of sorts; for me, suing the police meant affecting the community purse. So, that would never be for me.

Take any domestic arrangement that becomes abusive, it is really hard to leave it. Sad to say, I felt in the end that I was in a toxic relationship within my police career, one of us had to leave it.

I want you to leave this parable with a similar mentality. I want you to become your number one fan, mentor, sibling, and friend.

For it is you who is with you twenty-four-seven, three hundred and sixty-five days a year.

No one else.

The only standards you need to live by are your own.

And if it takes a bit of medication, therapy, and self-help to get you there – then so be it.

No one needs to know. Unless you want them to. What I have found though, is as soon as someone does tell their story, it has the propensity to offer someone else their salvation. So pray, please do story-tell.

I have high standards, I shouldn't have to adopt any less –

on the will of the majority say-so.

As for grief. It's a funny thing, grief.

Apparently, there are seven stages to it; bargaining, guilt, denial, anger, sadness, depression, and acceptance.

My experience is they jump around and repeat on you a bit, like a sour hiccup.

They aren't linear or neat, a bit like the jobs I attended throughout the course of my police career that spans over a decade, just shy of, unlucky for some, thirteen years. If I live to sixty-five, that's a fifth of my life there.

I'd do it all again, though. For definite. I was made for it.

I hadn't bargained for the mental toil it inevitably took on me. Not because of picking up after other people's loved ones from the tracks or dealing with people at their lowest ebbs. But because of siphoning my way through the myriad of challenges a rank-and-file organisation had in store for the likes of me.

"We need mentors that have managed to overcome the systems that we are born into," is what Comedian Russell Brand said in his Mentors book.

Comedy and a good sense of humour will see you through change. So, here I am. Writing this out.

Evidence of not just surviving through it, but now thriving from the experience. I feel like I *can* do or at least try anything.

There was no navigational book for the pitfalls of said system. I wasn't prepared to change my style or strong work ethic, because I had purpose there, I had mission – and I did it all as me, representative and part of a community I love and serve and will continue to serve until my dying early, middle, late, or night shift. To do it all whilst under immense strain of mental health conditions flaring up, I made a good effort in the end. Mentally incapable? I'll leave that for you to decide of me in the end. It is how one sergeant wrote about me to Occupational Health one day. There is a lot of stigma when it comes to mental health, I'm here to say it could happen to anyone – the stigma. Everyone has mental health.

What went well:
   The Book Thief: An unopened item of CCTV had no owner, so I had a look into it. It belonged to a copper who had resigned and left too. The job had been closed. I followed the line of enquiry, with only three days of oyster card enquiries left, I was able to identify the offender.

That didn't go so well:
   Work trousers made to split – Embankment station one day with two of my colleagues, I knelt down to pick up an item we were moving from A to B. My work trousers split. My colleagues were able to shield me all the way back to our station to replace the trousers. An arse covering exercise that was.

Side note: Is it a British thing? Unless in an elite dog unit or such like, police aren't permitted to wear shorts in hot weather. That itself is an injustice – one I lobbied to change, especially as we have hot weather like Australia (from time to time)!

Chapter 1
Bargaining

"You don't have to stick me on again. I've got another job."

This was Spring 2017. After yet another organisational re-shift, I had come 'unstuck' after replying to the inspector about a blue light driving course. At the time, I was in the process of putting together my BSc policing degree dissertation. Which I found a little bit time consuming and stressful.

My ex-husband was being deported as I had told the authorities of his precarious status on discovering I had been dating an illegal immigrant. Oops. Turns out this happens to a few of us cops. Love outside the police service at least. Some fall in love within it, or have affairs – that wasn't for me.

I think anyone who crosses borders for their family to have a better life could be marriage material. Was my personal view.

This was around the time when they said there was no neighbourhood police team any more.

"There is no neighbourhood police team any more," said the Response Sergeant.

The world around me was now seriously going mad. So, this became the time when I had to reexplain:

"You can't not have a neighbourhood police team, Sarge," I said to supervision – as 'the community is the police'.

A couple of weeks later, it was reintroduced as 'neighbourhood plus', or such like, and teams formulated literally out of nowhere.

Did someone senior seriously leave off 'community policing' in their proposed policing plan?

So, when it came to the blue light course for the Inspector I was able to speak to:

"How am I supposed to get the driving theory done, sir, if work isn't allocating me any time to get it done?"

All my spare time was being spent on a self-funded degree programme and policing dissertation. Equity is a term I learnt, about only taking what you need. I didn't need funding at the time to do that degree, so I didn't apply for any. I paid for it myself. I paid in time and money. I wasn't sure I had much else in reserve for *more*. I needed some help.

There wasn't any more time in a twenty-four-hour day for *more* police stuff, at that particular moment anyway. So that was my short, sharp, swift response to the Inspector, two rungs above me in the police chain – that would be my first and last opportunity to *ever* drive a police car with the lights on, he would reply.

He was right about that.

My plan B 'get out of jail' card was to become a part-time night tube operator for Transport for London (TfL). Plan A, to keep policing part-time as well.

Spreading myself between two occupations meant job security to me.

"No to that," said Professional standards.

So fight for that I did. But I had to leave first.

"Let me back in," I theoretically said as I re-applied to some interesting looking roles I'd be up for doing.

Only a couple of times.

I was rebuked by HR. Words to the effect, 'you've been out quite a while now'. The one face to face interview I did finally get, I was seven weeks pregnant at the time. No one wants you not operational and I didn't get the job.

I had previously failed my medical for a part-time post with the Met police (plan C); the chat went a bit like this with the psychiatric police service doctor,

"Doc, you must fail my medical if all that I have told you about would happen again here in the Met as well.

I'm trying to look after myself now".

Fail it for me they did then.

As for being allowed to do both occupations part-time, there are special constabulary tube drivers. I was asking to be paid for my contribution these days, please.

My police voluntary years were donated in my twenties. Now in my thirties, time was precious to me and had value when not spent at home. As home is the place I enjoy to be most of all. Any volunteering may fall around that.

I can't believe how I got that tube operator job whilst under enormous stress. I remember the interview.

"Why would you like to work for TfL"?

"I would like to work for a brand that I could represent at my best. Work to its core values, stand by TfL as a brand, and do my best for the brand."

Words to that effect, I got the job. The caveat to that being if the brand lives up to its entitlement of worthiness and praise.

Sometimes to know something or someone well, you have to join them. So here I am today, navigating through yet another impermeable, might as well be rank-and-file style organisation.

It's useful to know any foibles of the police are not unique to the police.

'Greenwashing' is a term used when organisations can be seen to be doing planet-friendly things. In reality, they are doing anything but. A phrase I learnt when doing a free online course through futurelearn.com.

In addition to greenwashing, I have seen the organisations that put up their Modern Slavery Statements. I have then watched cleaners unable to egress through barriered gates until a representative of the company presses them through.

Yet compare the modern slavery definition to their statement and its apparent the blatant discord, contradiction, and disregard to any meaningful support against such human-degrading atrocities. No one should be controlled by another, in any aspect of their life, working or otherwise.

I have seen companies display domestic abuse related posters, meant to aide employees. Yet, ask for flexible working to accommodate care related duties. You will find yourself with limited options, built around the way traditional nuclear families are seen, mostly with women left at the helm.

The problem-solving element question in the interview, I thought I had flunked.

"What would you do to solve a problem," they asked.

"Er, bit like flat-packed furniture building, start from the bit you have in front of you and work around it. Also, try and find the root cause and hopefully not only will you fix the problem right then and there, you'll also prevent reoccurrence."

Or words to that effect. That's me – stop it happening again.

I recall thinking I had absolutely nothing to lose in this interview.

They'd either hire me or they wouldn't.

Suicide was always a permanent solution for me to these temporary and often transient working-life problems. These working life problems had the propensity to propel any personal life problems to the fore as well.

Not entirely sure why suicide was my default position to go to, but it originates from being that small young child as a four or five-year-old strangling themselves, owing to frustration borne from being that round peg in a square hole at school. Yet another system made to educate the masses, not the few.

I find it fascinating that, whilst in the educational system, the careers advice signposts you towards quite typically institutional-type careers. For me, whilst in it, I had speech delay, and I think British Sign Language might have been a solution for me back then, if it had been an alternative form of taught 'spoken' word. Except its precluded at present from the UK national curriculum.

I quote 'because it's based on a world class model', or so the department of education tell me.

Except that world class model is predominantly exclusionary.

When I became a police officer for British Transport Police (BTP) in 2013, I had to complete my probationary period.

I failed one of the weeks of training yet passed with distinction, the highest accolade overall. I always had to put a little more effort in to get things.

"They'll have you out," were the voice echoes of a previous colleague I had the joy to work alongside, albeit briefly.

This was whilst I was working my notice as both police staff and a special constable for a Home Office Police service.

Everywhere I went, I seemed to 'upset' colleagues somehow.

I was happy to be at work mostly each day, for whatever challenge may come my way.

I was happy. They seemed not.

It's like all those unhappy people in positions of work they hate, yet they do nothing about their predicament.

I got stuck working my notice for an additional six months, as a premises who's licence I had successfully reviewed in conjunction with the licensing authority – for both underage drinking and noise complaints – went on to complain about me in turn. Oppressive, apparently. Yet how else does one show cause of a failing conduct? Other than methodically.

It was an inspector who said:

"You're not doing your job unless you're getting complaints."

He was right about that. Or just being kind.

Sometimes to make an omelette, you have to break eggs.

The professional standards team had incorrectly ticked the 'yes' box for 'open' complaints whilst returning my vetting status to BTP. The complaint had been finalised weeks earlier, it is their spreadsheet that hadn't. The consequence of that administrative error, and lack of information-checking, was time. The Windsor pay review and pension scale changes were kicking in UK wide. It's funny to me that they abolished 'special priority payments' or SPPs for tutor constables, yet tutor train operators still receive this additional bonus, and that is now where I am headed.

I think the police service was easy pickings when it came to this Windsor review. It's the same predicament nurses find themselves in. If you withdraw your labour – who suffers? The community. You are part of that community.

I would have to do an additional six months 'time' within an organisation I was ready to move on from. As well as a five-year additional pension and reduced starting salary. Oh well.

I've condensed two vocations into one now, let's see how *this* gig goes.

Within my new intake, a fellow officer had taken a similar path quite early on in their police career.

It was interesting that they had been labelled up as 'one of the ones to watch'. One destined for great things, like Superintendent, at least. When they told me they were leaving so early into their police career to be a tube driver, I was shocked. They were a natural. A good one.

It planted that correlated seed, that if they were doing that so early on, what had I missed? I was watching the one to watch all right. They left and so would I. This is the story of the unexpected consequences, namely feelings of relinquishing that career, which seems to fall impossibly neatly under the seven stages of grief. So similar to that as when a relationship breaks up or ends.

During my probation, and after a brief mandatory spell in a detective unit for my probationary portfolio, I returned from that spell to be given eight action plans by an up-and-coming, super fast-tracked acting sergeant to superintendent kind.

I had applied at the same time as them, out of competition, and failed my fast track to superintendent application.

I didn't really want it back then. I was competing against *them*. They were popular. I was not. I think I was trying to prove something to myself, to them, to everyone else. Not the greatest ingredients for success.

I shouldn't have applied for that reason alone. Only a superintendent is paid more than me, for now. I rose to the equivalent pay rank of superintendent; it just had to be outside the police service.

So when this fast track destined super issued me with my

eight action plans, it had been on the back of that I had told the old-sweat detectives I wouldn't be taking the custody paperwork home with me.

That I could still achieve, within the work-time hours, a paperwork 'drop off' at Finsbury Park BTP station on the route home. One of the old-sweats felt the need, whatever it was, to accompany me then all the way there. Like a chaperone.

I don't recall the content of our journey there. But I bet it was a *very* quiet one. I called and spoke to my DS friend, now a DI, about the eight action plans. They told me it was likely to be an exercise and to bin them, so I did. Regrettably, this meant I binned the evidence. HR looked blankly, when I requested to see them at a later date. The evidence would exist though, in that fast-tracked Super's higher echelon application process. One of the action plans contained the National Decision Making (NDM) model. It was the old version, so I pointed out the section in the middle was now replaced with ethics and we all continued along our merry ways.

I was already questioning peer level 'social norms' within my probation. On one occasion the neighbourhood Inspector wanted a chat. It was a minute before the shift was due to end and whilst we often gave half an hour free to HM service. A chat would be better served at the beginning of the shift – or like I had seen them with other colleagues anytime between. I piped up again, it wasn't the right time.

This wouldn't be the first or last time for me to question 'social norms', for it became a thing to regularly dine out together or else, again, set yourself apart as different, as difficult, as the one not to be trusted within the team.

All I was trying to do instead was safeguard the team and not repeat previous mistakes. When one cop balls up, it reverberates on. Like a basketball that loses steam after its first high bounce. It reverberates and bounces down and down and down. Any balls-up only ever really affects the front-line and always with an extra layer of bureaucracy from then on in. It became apparent that these layers were fruitless, however, when time and time again, many jobs still did get overlooked. Or worse, as a result of the layers, your case ends up failing in court.

When the judge asks me:

"Officer, why has this simple theft case taken so long to end up in this court."

It's unprofessional to say because of all the layers of bureaucracy it had to get through to get here. Added with a little incompetence. We're meant to all run with it.

The system and process took so long. I was doing all I could each time.

We were always given investigations, twenty to thirty to manage, even though we were response, but no accreditation to be a detective. You were restricted even more.

I wouldn't describe myself as having a remit.

I'd take any job going.

I would find myself cleaning the offices sometimes, so we would have a clear desk policy to begin working through the next crate of work or handover. Even if it was a cleaner's role, I was more than prepared to do what it took to get the job done. From the bottom up. I still do the cleaner's job now. I clean rubbish off the train, so they don't have as much, and it also prevents items becoming trapped in the doors. That effects the efficient running of that public service I am now in. I tend to get on well with fellow grafters. My belligerence is often how new introductions forge.

An organised office leads towards an organised investigation. One day, another officer did a search on how many jobs other officers seemed to have. I had learned by then not to concern myself too much with what other colleagues may or may not be up to. They're still in the police now. They're a character, working alongside one of my very good university friends.

There are many more female police officer tales to be shared. Those two both have even longer careers.

I hope they share them. Many would read them. When you're in the police, you're scared to say anything out of turn. They don't seem to want me back, so what have I got to lose?

As a result of their inquisitive nature. It transpired, some of the other officers, had only four investigations, if any.

They had four to be able to respond to any job at the drop of a hat on blue lights in response. I wanted that. I wanted four jobs and to respond to jobs on blue lights for a bit. I didn't want twenty to thirty investigations then to run there on a bunioned foot.

Why couldn't they have had twenty to thirty jobs and also respond on blue-lights? I would've had to. It was funny how when I applied to re-join as a part-time detective to be told I didn't have the credentials.

More often than not, my cases resulted well and were at least detected. All of which accounts for nothing on paper now. You are not a detective (DC). Only ever a police constable (PC) trained. That's OK, too. I tried.

I wanted to do my job to the best of my ability, is all.

I wasn't needing to concern myself with arse-covering exercises or 'what's in it for me' accreditations, I was getting on with the work ahead of me. I was task-focussed.

Focussed, methodical, and relentlessly on a learning path. The victim on this failing court case had been shoved to the ground during night tube and their property strewn, passer's by assisting – but the one opportunistic alleged thief, spotting their opportunity, took the phone off the ground.

Incredibly, station CCTV then showed them permanently deprive the victim of their goods and pocket it. I had secured their whole route home pretty much with the phone. CCTV wasn't enough, though – a combination of a prosecuting barrister's first day; a shit-hot defence barrister. Was it my failure not to say about how bureaucratic it had been to get it there? To elicit sympathy. Through supervision, quality control, decision making, crown prosecution service (CPS), and all these channels working isolated from each other and all the way back again… back to me… back to all the audiences; the group of victims, suspects, and witnesses to update… don't shoot the messenger!

But I got it to court.

Everyone involved in that case taught me something. As I was seeing it from all sides of the event.

The judge proper poo-pooed it, though. Two years of work gone and an unhappy victim in the end.

I couldn't have done more.

I wasn't supposed to be there that day, I turned up uninvited by the courts' system to see it through.

Some of the cases being heard that day, the defendants whose officer on case were also not invited to attend, needed some attending to. My hands were full again. Paramedics attended. It was a party.

One of the reasons I made that final leap of faith to leave was choice. We all have them. It can be difficult to make a decision, however. I can leave work this day, never to return, and return home to my family, who all the while showed love and support unconditionally. I am super grateful for having them.

"Thank you for existing." is something we say often in our home.

It's a really sad environment each day to go into somewhere where your type or style is not welcome or wanted. Whereas at home, amongst close friends, I was. It was this incompatibility that made me think I can try other things. I am by my own side now. I don't need others' endorsement.

Turns out though, people and colleagues can be just as mean in other professions too. I've had some therapy to get over this. I left the therapy when we concluded it really is OK to continue to be kind and nice in an otherwise hostile world of trolls.

Yes, I will probably continue to be disappointed by the unkind words and actions of others. They're figuring out their life, I suppose, and how others fit into it. I've managed to figure out mine, I hope they can and you can too, if you haven't figured it out already. There is a lot of injustice in the world, it bothers me. It bothers me when more can be done, but isn't.

The last job I attended to was a wanted-on warrant missing person. Within ten minutes, I had found them, not even visibly on display but underneath their sleeping bag. 'You are here' was so eloquently stated on the map they were laid underneath.

No other officer in two weeks could find them, but I knew how to. Except, I wasn't technically allowed in the end to get on and do my job.

I was very much present in what I would make my very last job. A very senior officer had decreed me for 'restricted duties only', no explanation. I will come to that at the end of this story.

My world opened up on leaving the police. Much to my dismay, I came across working for a police colleague who had been sacked.

Their bad day became their career ending move. A career long endeavour ended overnight. The media would villainise them and demonise them. The media were often key in getting key messages out. The master of the arts, they are one firm never to underestimate.

I had always thought myself destined to a career in professional standards. Sacking 'bad cops'. I would relish in that I would have thought. Especially when one of them told me about slamming on the brakes whilst driving prisoners around.

"It must have been a fox after all."

That could easily be you or me in there some day.

It had been me on one occasion.

In 2008, I was training to be a special constable when on a night out, separated from my friends and sozzled, I spotted the police in the leisure park.

To my delight, I went over to share that I too was 'one of them'. I'm a special constable you know!

The response I got wasn't as high spirited as mine, so I challenged this by saying:

"That's not how you should be speaking to people."

I guess it went from there. I must have quarrelled. A fine ingredient of being drunk. Or twenty, female, and confident.

I was then bundled into a police van, handcuffed behind my back, left in an asphyxiating position with my top falling down, and driven around for what felt like ages. Speed bump, after speed bump, after speed bump. It wasn't until years later, when this cop said about slamming the brakes on for 'annoyingly loud' prisoners, I realised that it had been going on for years.

A welcome committee was at custody, never have I ever seen so many uniforms in one place as I did that day.

I am not even built like a brick shit house. Although I do contain as much sometimes and urgently.

When my moment with the custody sergeant came, I leant over and whispered in my best sober voice:

"There really is no need for all these people."

And with that, he dismissed them all.

Yes, I could and should have put a complaint in at the time, but I had been drunk. I took full responsibility for that fact, no one else had got me sozzled – but I have always remembered that arrest so well. It proved useful, that experience, in the end, when drunk men in my licensing jurisdiction started turning up, calling police for assistance having been beaten up and left abandoned – it was their first lines in the calls I recognised so clearly from my own experience of being 'drunk'.

You say it so clearly, then doubt yourself, as drink eats at your memory of events. Each job of theirs I saw kept being closed down, one after the other.

No victim complaint, no crime investigation.

No victim, no crime. In the muse of Bob Marley.

It was night-time economy related.

I stretched my remit to cover this otherwise uncovered set of events.

Call for service, man after man, descriptions started coming and I began piecing them together.

It was door staff who were the assailant, but where.

Which premises was taking their punters off pitch for a beating elsewhere? It wouldn't be long before one of these men ended up dead or involved in a road traffic collision.

I recall one of them was even dumped the other end of town by a service station about three miles away from where I concluded the unlicensed door staff were originating from. You know who's going to get the blame for this?

The night clubs, I thought.

They are going to get the blame for all these curtilage drunks. As soon as someone else picks up the dots I already had. All the door staff at the night clubs were legitimate, as far as I could tell, as were the other establishments in the area. The clubs and premises were, generally speaking, really well run.

That's when I approached the community Pubwatch for their help.

I said to the group:

"Now, I know this is none of you… but I need your help please."

From that weekend on, every premises (just shy of thirty) in the Pubwatch worked with me and was submitting a list of their door staff log in numbers.

I checked their validity against the security industry authority (SIA) register. As predicted, all licensed and above board.

In doing so, I was then able to ask for those premises that who, as a hunch of mine, would be operating without licensed door staff. In plain sight, if a licensed premises had door staff on the door, where was their register of sign ins please?

Even now I walk about and can tell the difference between a well-run establishment and one that is not.

I am that random one person who calls in to report that there is a water leak down that road, or a fire exit is locked or blocked. I do it from learning of disasters where people were not as lucky to have someone do just one more thing for them.

A well-run establishment has its house-keeping sorted.
When it came to these closed incidents.
Oh, I see. I made myself officer in case (OIC).

It didn't take long, working with the Pubwatch group. A couple of weekends for this unlicensed door staff hypothesis to work out. The solution to our problem was not to hold anyone to account, there were no forthcoming victims. The solution was to get licensed door staff on and prevent further kicking ins.

The after-hours kicking ins then stopped, word must have got round that the police licensing officer was sniffing around. The premises got licensed door staff and kicked out the deadwood. There really was no place for this style of beating within the night-time economy – not in this town.

After that, the Pubwatch got updated, no longer had to submit a copy of the SIA door staff sign in sheets to me, and got thanked for their cooperation. I think I had sold for their buy in by telling them that, if they didn't help me, one of them would be getting the responsibility for all those after-hours kick ins eventually. I also think they cared about their customers. Deeply. So when I go on to say:

"No one died on my watch."

This is what I mean by that.

The system would have let call after call, beaten up after beaten up man, falling under no one's remit, be continually overlooked. Until one of them ended up beyond repair.

Then it would have gone on someone else's remit, depending on who ended up killed or seriously injured.

Then the town would have been labelled as deleteriously broken, as it was already starting to get labels from a reality TV show. It wasn't and never was deleterious. It was up and coming. Pubwatch proved that. We were a team.

Conversely, it was during a licensing meeting where I was most at risk of bother – and not from the licensees.

An elected councillor walked straight up to me and pulled and yanked my hair so hard, to see if my hair was real. I wore a smart suit, my hair tied up, but it was long and plenty.

It hurt a lot and left me with a headache.

I was too polite to do anything about it. In a room full of other meeting delegates, I brushed it off. Their excuse was they were a hairdresser. The inspector at the time was on point – afterward he asked if I wanted anything done about that. Just a word, gov, might do – in that councillor's ear.

The opportunity of that licensing officer post gave rise to a unique experience, purely and solely on the back of a reality TV show. It would give so many unique and exciting opportunities for that community, and I am grateful for that opportunity and my time there. Prior to another police reform hitting our screens.

In 2010, I had landed the above new role as police staff in a job previously undertaken by police sergeants. It had been civilianised. At the same time, a club reopened and the reality show had launched. Simultaneously.

It was an unprecedented time.

I was in the thick of it and loved it.

In the height of counterterrorism, a patrol unit had responded to a call of such substance, with an 'area search no trace' response. The incident had been closed. Except, it was my role to trawl all licensing-related incidents and attribute them or deny them to the licensed premises concerned and take appropriate action where necessary.

I think looking into a bunch of young, drunk men getting their heads and bodies kicked in was appropriate action.

An important factor I discovered in investigations was sometimes it was satisfying disproving someone's guilt, especially in the cases that were of a vexatious kind.

Tit for tat, or such like.

My role included fighting off wrongly attributed incidents, especially when it came to the clubs. Incidents attributed wrongly to landmark's occurred fairly frequently and sometimes understandably so. Accuracy is an important part of building up any picture of a situational representative (sit rep).

Incidents may occur on the street outside, usually as a result of one of the feeder-bar premises, owing to irresponsible drinks deals. A difficult aspect to the management of a night-time economy beast to tame and address. But address I would try. Address the root cause of any issue was always my objective, to stem the flow of jobs. Here lay the red flags. I was a hawk for a red flag. Red flag number 1: member of public informant had watched male covertly recording. The camera was under a jumper, or so it seemed. Red flag number 2: the licensed premises was a very British place hosting plenty of Sports events. Red flag number 3: reality TV show land. Red flag number 4: key locations with commuter transport links.

A reality show that glamourised lifestyle. It would have enemies. Just like they purport through the relationship interactions on their show. Nothing happened in the end. But only because I spent the remainder of that afternoon and evening chasing down who to show my investigation results to. The TV show to me was an interesting addition to my jurisdiction. This was extra 'curriculum' thus learning material for me.

There were resident-style complaints, how the show was changing the area. All I could identify was the opportunity for growth and opportunities for that town. I wanted to support that rising tide of opportunity and change. Fundamental to community success is good foundations and opportunities within it. So, let that licence be granted! The initial responding officer to the area search landed himself in trouble afterward. But only because he shouted at me for undermining his initial response. The inspector intervened on that one. Nothing happened, though. The show remains on our screens. But someone did eventually die.

I was privileged to work alongside an entrepreneur, who instructed about their person all the very best of the business assets.

I had cause to visit the premises and speak with the designated premises supervisor weekly, sometimes fortnightly, whatever was needed or required to get the job or weekend events done.

To rebuke that 'CLOSE THAT CLUB DOWN'. I did that job, 2010-2013, and the premises seemed to come off the screens after that coincidentally.

The whole experience remains to date one of the most unique experiences I can ever recall being involved with.

An opportunity that the premises owner themself created, of which I was collateral experience.

Their suicide was of deep sadness to me when I discovered this news. How can someone so kind, giving so many opportunities to people within the community, die in such a way, alone. I hope they are in comfort and peace now. It's not fair and it's not OK. They are another stat lost to the preventable death by suicide. You never know what someone else may be dealing with. Had I have followed direction to 'close the club down', that suicide could have occurred as a result of police oppression. As it occurred so many years later, it may be fair to say it seems not.

What went well:
On a bus one day, I noticed a symbol I was not familiar with on a Church. On asking the Church about it, they had no knowledge of it being there and confirmed they hadn't put it there. The symbol is used to mark buildings for terrorist attacks.

That didn't go so well:
Rookie error... wrote the wrong month on a fixed penalty notice. So they got off it. As I was issuing it in the middle of the night, I resolved to always wear a Casio watch to outline the day, date, time, and year. It helped.

Chapter 2
Guilt

The moments when I attempted suicide in my life, I will not refer to at great lengths. Namely, I am a strong advocate not to share suicide methodology, or how those attempts were made. For it is for a very unwell person to store 'successful' methodology, if not for the immediacy of now, but for later. All that remains to be said is a vivid image of my grandparents came to my fore – perhaps at the moment when it see-sawed to the point of almost becoming too late to stop what had been my intentional act to end my own life.

Suicide is not one isolated issue, it's a culmination of issues – no one person is responsible for it, even the patient themselves isn't in the healthiest frame of mind. It comes down to ingredients like empathy, compassion, and kindness to combat it. We've all got the potential in us, but we need to offer it up first to ourselves, then work out from there.

It was in that instance I chose to live, continue to survive, and maybe even aim to thrive one day. If I'm honest, I imagined being happy one more time, then doing it whilst happy. I was surprised then to learn that suicide can tend to occur during the 'upward turn'. So, this vivid image of upsetting my grandparents, I couldn't pass any pain on to the elderly. I find it hard to pass any pain on to anyone if I can stop it.

I'm proud to say now, it was the best decision I made to stick around. Nothing else compares to it really. Life is a gift, a unique opportunity to lift off any glass ceiling and say, 'I really can do anything I set my heart and mind to achieving'. Or at least have fun in the process and journey leading close enough to it.

Everyone has their struggles from time to time, sometimes it lasts for years, but as a famous saying goes, 'there is a younger version of yourself that is so proud of you' – or words to that effect.

The only thing you've got to do is keep competing in your own life. But only towards your own standards, being kind and accepting to yourself the whole time. Be grateful to yourself, then others.

As I said to a still serving colleague recently, no one is going to say 'Well done' to you. No one. So you are going to have to say it to yourself. Well done. I am so proud of you. I'm going to say thank you to you. I am going to say, you tried. Well done. Sometimes I even do a train announcement like this. Saying well done and thank you to everyone on board. Who else is going to thank them and say well done for being there?

As for the premises owner, they were one of the rare people who even tried to say thank you to me. They bought me a hamper that first Xmas – which the Inspector said I could not accept. I listened. I politely explained how I couldn't accept it, that I hoped for one of their staff to benefit from it instead. But the sentiment remains in my heart and mind today. What I didn't listen to was a Superintendent at the time, who balled into the office I shared at the time with an administrator – the administrator who never spoke to you unless you were male – the super telling me to shut the premises down if I wanted my name in lights. It seems both my name and vehicle weren't destined for lights in the police.

Doing things 'my way', I would say reasonably – instead of their way led me to recently design some British Sign Language alphabet pages. Showing the signs from both angles as "you sign", "I sign". A lot of policing is about perspectives. Creativity can be therapy for those with alternative mindsets.

Step ahead and do it first in front of them as a leader.

Mentor. Tutor. Show people how you want to be shown.

So by going against the grain, I became the bad apple metaphor.

"Get the bad apples out."

There was a time when I thought that would be my most sought-after position within the police, professional standards. Go after them as hard as I ever did the perpetrators of any of my crime investigations et al. Line of duty anyone?

"Go, go, go!"

Except the whole while, I was the bad apple, or so it was made to seem. It certainly was how I was treated. I was challenging the brotherhood. The thin blue line.

So, when I came to meet an officer that had been sacked, it presented an entirely new concept to me. Being human. Despite being one and working all around them.

There presented for me this whole grey area. This whole, complete person who had been sacked from the police service. How very nice this always to be ex-cop colleague friend would be. A nice and not at all bad person, ex-cop.

They had simply made a catalogue of career ending gaffes, all at the same time. The media bayed for blood, the family bayed for blood – and they got it. The officer lost their job. At least. No regard for all their previous work or service, which again spanned well over a decade. They were made an example of.

That is how I see their experience. Made to be an example, to be 'talked about', but only when they were not around to defend themselves in yet another canteen-style culture room – this time by tube drivers, whose careers sometimes spanned over impressive forty year turns by choice. A similar rhetoric you see in many professions, the police are no different – they often offer their experience.

This ex-colleague 'sacked' cop was cast out, without any regard for them being human too. Human to perhaps be themselves, in need of a little encouragement as they headed towards the next phase of their life, chapter, and new beginnings. Outside of the police.

Fortunately, they made it somehow. I admire them for doing so, clearly abandoned and alone from this brotherhood and thin blue line. They became my one to watch.

I call what happened to them 'pain-transferring'.

It's a bit like when that teacher blames a parent for their misbehaving child, when instead the teacher is not accepting responsibility for their role. The teacher could say instead, "I don't know how to manage your child. But that doesn't mean I won't find out how to or at the very least try."

There was a well-liked and revered sergeant once, who said I was mentally incapable of being a police officer to occupational health, instead of them questioning their own abilities and saying, "I don't know how to best manage this PC."

Instead, the blame was shifted on from them to me – the 'problem'. A bit like pain. It was passed on as someone else's problem to try and fix. Except I didn't need fixing, I needed understanding and to find my place within the system.

I am not saying the pain felt by the police service, the loved ones, or society as a whole, can excuse poor or shoddy police work. But it is a subject I became aware of when I reported a significant incident that occurred to me in the least suspecting circumstances.

The choices were inexplicable, but I understood them. I had this opportunity to absorb the pain all for myself, instead of transferring it onto other humans. When it came to my choice, I chose to absorb the pain and not further risk inflicting it upon other people. That's where pain can cease.

I guess it's a difficult process to imagine, forgiveness, empathy, and understanding, until you're placed in that position yourself. I'm confident in my choice though.

It still hurts, though, like every error the police ever made where society suffered as a result.

In a proposed policing model I drew up one day, these learning themes would forever stick out like sharp corners and points that will forever hurt when you prick against them. They hurt now, as much as they ever did – and we cannot forget them. I am talking about Racism: Stephen Lawrence. Misogyny: Alice Ruggles. Corruption: Daniel Morgan. Homophobia: as depicted by BBC's Four lives – Anthony Walgate, Gabriel Kovari, Daniel Whitworth, and Jack Taylor. I have the utmost respect for their families' unimaginable battles.

What seemed to me to be a common theme from the loved ones left behind, was their drive for others in any community, not to experience the same pain as they are going through, to prevent another family experiencing their experience. Not exclusively, but these echo within society as well. With full knowledge of all these events making the police look very *very* bad as an institution. These events require deep, introspective change from within the police service, as individuals, both in and out of it.

Having read Dr Gwen Adshead's book, 'The devil you know', in their experience when dealing with complex individuals in treatment suites, there is always a reason for someone's worst day. A culmination of events, and the impact on others it can go on to have is magnificent.

I wonder then, how we can transfer Dr Adshead's understanding mentality to the beast that is itself a conglomerate organisation, consisting of individuals and competing parts.

Why should I be the only person looking out for water leaks, blocked fire escapes, and signs of trouble within my community. Don't we all want that peace and security?

To some extent, could it be fair to surmise society can act like a mirror? We all as individuals continue to have to work longer, harder and all for less. Yet still together amongst historical mistakes of the many, in the sake of following the crowd mentality, sometimes we all just go along with the flow. I am glad this ex-police colleague managed to navigate their way through the career-ending experience. For any diligent officer, to be sacked from duty is a fate unimaginable to its core. They're a great manager of people now.

It is one experience we all fear enough to want to do the job properly in the first place. Speaking from experience anyway.

It comes down to humiliation as well, and public humiliation at that. We talked of that feeling of being ashamed together, ashamed it happened, ashamed to say it happened, ashamed to say what others could make of it. To imagine what others will make of you.

I had been ashamed to say I was in the police to many who asked what I did for a living. Feeling ashamed is in the family of words for feeling guilty.

People use your police service against you too. They say things like, "I thought you were in the police," discouragingly. Just because you might not know something.

Yet as you will come to know or soon discover, it is

irrelevant what others make of you or your *one* bad day. For them to judge your life-time on that *one* occurrence, *one* mistake, or catalogue or chain of events. The very human nature and condition that makes us human in the first place, is that we all make mistakes or expansive misjudgements, we live and learn by them. Where there is a willingness to.

If ever an example laid bare of a story that should be shared and told, it is their story. Their story of recovery from being sacked. They won't be the first, and they won't be the last. That's for sure. Maybe you are even reading this as you find yourself having been sacked from your previous occupation. It doesn't make you a bad person, being sacked. It makes you precariously human. I hope I have shared their story well enough to give someone else some hope.

They're doing well now.

It took them a while, but they got there.

One thing was clear in the police. If you made your sergeant's job easier, by not creating them work to do, you were on their pleasantry list. You would get on all right within the organisation as well. Get opportunities to grow and expand your career.

In the end, I had revised for a search course I had been promised for it to then not materialise.

I had studied for a tutor course for it to again not materialise. Every door closing, every door open seemingly to everyone else, with a supervisor's endorsement attached to it.

Just not mine, without an exception to the rule which occurred in around 2011, when I was the first special constable to do placement on a detective unit, monitoring what TV programmes are now made of as documentaries. Monitoring the most violent and sexual offenders as they reintegrate back into their communities.

A detective sergeant (DS) had helped me get a Counter

terrorism (CT) job to special branch that I had detected and he had come across me working late as police support staff.

If you never answered back, did what you were told, and never questioned upwards, you would get on all right. Maybe even thrive. You would get on all right on occasions if you got lucky and met a mutually like-minded soul within the ranks. This occurred rarely. It did however happen right up until the end of my career, and I recall one of my sergeants getting upset about how bad they felt they had treated me. They put me under the wing of a mentor, who deserves a knighthood for all the other things they have done for others in their career.

Joining a 'rank and file' organisation, you would think that would be clear.

You're there to follow orders until you're in a position to dish out the orders.

I hadn't joined the army. Although their motto rings true: 'Be the best'. Reach your full potential. It would take me over a decade to understand what this meant within what seemed on the outside as a warm and fuzzy, funny family. But never ever defy rank or file. Or else.

I always *tried* to do what I was told. It is just what I was being told to do, or not do sometimes seemed to be or feel a bit wrong or off in some way. And I always came back with evidence as to why that was the case.

Being that round peg in a square hole, and now placed on forced restrictions, I had to undergo a series of psychological tests for autism, ADHD, and dyslexia.

I passed for autism and dyslexia. That is, I have these extra special skills that mean I think more diversely and, quite often, won't just 'get it'. I have to find my own way, that would be clear. But these can act as super problem-solving powers. Some of my personal successes and resilience is credited to them.

I credit it as why I consider myself to be 'retired' and still in my thirties. I didn't clock on to policing and leave my personality at the door. I didn't change on entering the police service, they would try to change me. Except they couldn't because I was made this way.

I wasn't the one who needed changing either.

It is why I have concluded part of the solution to policing could be to remove the rank and file from operations. Divorce the rank and file.

Gradually phasing out rank to be replaced with one community level officer.

But who would tell you to do your job?

You shouldn't need to have to be told in the first place, you should be there because you want to be there and be driven to do it. Co-ordination is all that may be required.

I propose that's the significant change that is needed.

"Defund the police," some chant.

There is another way, and let's all keep working together to find workable solutions on this community endeavour. Leaving no one behind, everyone included in it.

You're as strong as your weakest team member, apparently.

In order to do that, we must face, head on, all of the good, all of the bad, and all of the ugly within policing and the community. That's what this parable may be a catalyst for and has resolved for me.

What went well:

A suspect committing a racist public order offence, dropped a piece of paper, which got identified within the rubbish from CCTV review. As a team working together to decipher the piece of paper, it led to their arrest near-by.

That didn't go so well:

Rookie error... Undercover lover. Disagreed with a City of London Police officer on a job. They asked to speak to a supervisor, so my plain-clothed colleague said they were the supervisor and the problem disappeared.

Chapter 3
Denial

The mention of the psychological at work had begun in 2008. When after a year of financial processing as police staff in a Home Office police service, I had been promoted into a new role to process and reconcile the overtime of officers.

As well as monitor that all important council tax hotline, often written in small text on the annual council tax bulletin.

Be assured, at least one member of the community would always ring it, annually, to ask what they might expect from the police that year. They probably were the mystery shopper, to be honest with you. At least, I suspected they were.

I had been encouraged to apply and go for this promotion, having detected a way to save the police service money. I had achieved this by way of overdue invoices and associated late payment charges.

It was daft, all these companies had ginormous fees for late payments, and as an organisation, we would ordinarily approve the budget and keep paying them.

Rather than anyone think to tackle or address any root cause of any payment issues. I treated the organisation as if it were my own precious budget. No one to bail me out, no one to give me a hand out. Totally responsible for every penny.

For me, I had always treated every penny as if it were three. You find a penny, your bank stays the same, you take a penny off your shop and spend one penny less from your pocket. Every penny is worth three to me. The pennies soon become pounds, and the pounds can buy you things. Like a place to call home.

My Grandad was rendered speechless when, as a ten-year-old me, he tried to impart his wisdom to me – he said:

"The first one thousand pounds is the hardest."

To which I replied:

"Grandad, I have already saved ten thousand pounds."

At ten years of age, I had amassed a savings account equivalent to my age. Ask any person with experience on their side, there isn't much that renders them completely speechless.

My grandparents have long held a sign on reception to their home. It reads, 'Live long enough to be a problem to your children, grandchildren, and great grandchildren'. Mine might have read, 'Live long enough to be a problem to your seniors'.

School wasn't teaching me finance. I was learning it vicariously through what I was observing all around me the whole time, through the self-employed mentality. I was learning it for myself and not ignoring signs of working towards my future destiny. When I left school, I remember writing them feedback about the lack of financial awareness, that I feared for my peers going forward 'automatically' into university and a wall of debt.

So, when I identified *'my'* organisation, the magnificent police service, needlessly paying all these overdue bills,

"Not on my watch," I thought.

It was down to the 'cut off' system in place. If the authorised for payment invoice wasn't in the finance department's tray by three p.m. Friday, it would not make the bank (BACS) cut off the following Tuesday. Budget controllers were making the payment deadlines, it was this extra week delay that was causing all the bother.

"What about Monday?" I would ask.

"We are working through all the invoices Monday and inputting them. And there has to be a cut off."

It was the way it was and had been for many years. So along came a Monday and I counted the number of overdue invoices left in the 'cut off' tray. Secretly and covertly.

Let's say there was fifty out of one hundred. There's five of us on the team… that's an extra ten each – doable right?

To prove my point. I did my workload, then this extra fifty myself, alone. I could touch type thanks to my Dad, so I touch-typed faster.

I did this for a couple of weeks to show it wouldn't be a manageable 'one off' change.

Because I showed this to work, everyone else became up for it. Thumbing through the invoice cut-off tray after three p.m. on a Friday felt good. There was no electric pulse for sticking your hand in the tray after the cut-off point or deadline.

Taking on only a few more each week, eventually this whittled down to almost none. It was a self-feeding issue. Overdue payments decreased from that week on.

A budget holder or two became relieved. A chief accountant became pleased.

There would always be overdue *'overdue'* ones – but ultimately I would receive a letter of acknowledgement for my endeavour when the time came for me to move to the other end of the office and take on this promotional seat. I was flying high.

Except it became a nightmare.

The manager I was under was cantankerous.

"Know your remit, girl," they would bark.

"I don't have a remit, I get the job, any job that needs doing, done."

The phone would ring, I would sort that officer's conundrum out.

"I am police staff."

"I am police <u>support</u> staff."

I bolster the operational officers, so they can do what they do best and police. That was my *expectation* of my role and remit.

At this point in time, I hadn't plans to become an operational police officer myself.

I had plans to become a chartered (CIMA) accountant.

I was good with money. Mine and others. If they let me be.

I couldn't pass the CIMA assessments though. There seemed to be no feedback on what questions I was getting wrong in the multiple-choice questions (MCQs). I only did the exam a couple of times to know I was wasting my time and should change tact.

"You don't tell them their bank details, it's for them to tell us their bank details," this manager said to me whilst on this phone call.

When you've got a superintendent ringing you up, and you can blatantly see they've passed over the sixteen-digit long card number instead of their bank details, *it is my job* to say something.

To solve their problem as police <u>support</u> staff.

To steer them to the right area on their card.

I worked for HSBC previously, albeit briefly. I knew their cards and they were an HSBC customer.

This poor superintendent had already called up before, or so they told me. Funnily, I had started within the organisation with bounties of respect and admiration for the rank.

I knew a superintendent was very high up.

So why hadn't it been sorted for them? Why was someone this high up having all this bother? They had other more pressing matters to be getting on with, I would have thought.

Why hadn't it been sorted then.

They hadn't spoken to me yet.

They had probably spoken to the only other person in this section of the office. And that person was becoming a real pain in my amygdala.

By the end of that call to the super, I had sorted it. They would be paid whatever it was that they were due and that would be the end of that. One less call later on was my work mentality. If you don't teach someone properly how to do something, how can they be expected to know? My work mentality wasn't welcomed here. In this corner of an otherwise proficient and wonderful working office.

The mood had now changed.

People too afraid to get involved and say anything. To say they see the change in an otherwise proactive colleague's demeanour.

It began like this.

Then continued with this manager making insidious and snidey comments about my work, destroying my paperwork, and not saying anything about it – instead left it for me to come across when looking for it. No areas for improvement identified for me to work on, which might have been the inevitable, especially when starting a new promotional grade, as I had done.

It then moved on to my time-keeping. For example, I would have my break at twelve noon, let's say. After a glorious walk around the police headquarters grounds, I would return and be sat at my desk by 12:27 p.m. The computer always took a couple of minutes to log back in. To this day, most institutional computers still do. I was punctual. As ever. *I loved my job, I loved working there* and *I loved my life* up until this point.

When I returned recently to the grounds, it's amazing how much smaller they seem.

In my memory, the windows I had looked out from, and my time there, had been much more larger than the reality of life or how it at least seems today.

Today it is even fenced in.

This 12:27 p.m. incident.

"You're late," they said.

Except this time it was said closer than ever before, they had snuck up behind me and barked it quietly in my ear.

No one else apparently watching or seeing this. I felt their breath. I smelt their body. I hadn't heard their approach. I hadn't expected them. Up until that point, I had wrongly thought I would be safe at this work place, within the confines of the police environment. I was now on my own and felt it.

I think this is when the psychological doors creaked ajar.

I can even recall that moment of 'freezing' in utmost terror.

I am not safe anywhere.

This happened again when in BTP, on a bank holiday deployment. I fatally wore an orange scrunchy in my hair and the public order deployment stab vest. I got shouted at and belittled for it. I wasn't expecting danger at that immediate point by a colleague again.

Public, I was all ready for a bit of spittle shouting. That never upset me or got to me. Shout in my face, fine. Stranger.

It's when its someone I know, I don't react to a plan.

After this incident, I left the public order unit as it sat too similar to the unsafe anywhere notion. That was like a trigger again. Having done it for only a year, alongside neighbourhood policing, I still have fond memories of sitting in the van round the corner from a public order-ish event.

The public order sergeant even made me dump my coffee in situ, not even putting my litter in the bin.

"Drop it now, we are going."

We moved in sequences, like when you see formations of birds in the sky migrating. Together. I liked that sergeant. I don't think they liked me.

Thinking of that now, that's quite a juxtaposition of roles. A friendly neighbourhood police officer with public order shield and baton wielding cordon language 'GET BACK' and 'WELCOME TO YOUR NEIGHBOURHOOD'.

The public order training had been a hoot to boot. It was abundantly clear why I was there, they always needed more women in it.

I was papped in a cordon one time in that otherwise anonymous public order looking unit, that time outside London Bridge. There had been a suspicious package and the station had gone into evacuation mode.

For whatever reason now, that media image is no longer available on the internet to recover. If it did still exist somewhere out there, it would fall neatly under a section in the library of 'women in period costumes, facing away'.

Yet more evidence I played my part in maintaining a suffragette ethos and movement forward undeterred by barriers.

I likened leaving the police to getting out of a domestic relationship. A bit like filing for divorce.

I had been in a pretty bad relationship, prior to joining the police service as staff.

It was complicated.

Everything was invested in this one relationship. No other future existed.

Except the other party wasn't there for your best interest, for you to thrive.

They were there to sap the very life out of you if they could.

It sounds easy to walk away from that; how horrendous it would be to stay.

But ask anyone in a domestic arrangement like this, it never can be as simple as that. You're living in denial the whole time. I think it's why I have come to the conclusion that there begins the bereavement of sorts, the severed tie and finality of a relationship that you thought you had signed up *for life*.

There was no denying it on leaving it, policing was my life.

This book is not about casting aspersions on the police service.

Or any individual.

The police service is made up of individual people.

There were, however, from my experience within it, so many of those arse-covering, own-arse-saving leaders and front-line operatives alike.

Yet it is just a job at the end of the day, just a job and you will be replaced tomorrow.

Especially if the organisation decides not to need you in *that* post for whatever reason any more.

If an occasion came up where you felt like you were risking your job, in turn your livelihood, for doing the right thing. In not taking that risk in *doing the right thing*. You could well end up sacked not for doing the right thing anyway, and lose your job. So get on and do the right thing. My single piece of advice to impart on anyone still serving in the police would be to continually always do the right thing. Even when no one is watching you, and especially when it may seems like the hardest thing you could be doing.

You don't know which time it will pay off.

Do it.

Follow that hunch, that gut instinct, and lead.

Importantly, do that extra enquiry here and there.

You can always smell the bagel shop and the comradery at another time. Because in that time, that member of the public, member of your community, with their enquiry presented before your snout, might not get another opportunity again for your intervention or friendly advice.

Do what the job you're in requires of you. Just do one more thing usually.

In 2017, when the atrocity of the Manchester arena bombings happened, it was astonishing that on reading the dossier and breakdown of events afterwards, that there was a missed opportunity to save all those innocent souls' lives. If only a cop had walked up to the suicide bomber apparently. That seemed to be all that was needed, or so I garnered from that report.

There would have been far less casualties and deaths incurred. Who knows, maybe if the cop could even level with someone wearing a suicide vest, a young man, could it have been enough for the young man to change his mind, in turn to land on the equivalent Dr Adshead seat?

If a negotiator can negotiate, who knows.

We will never know.

Because history is written on what *did* happen.

It is far harder to say what didn't happen, or didn't occur.

For the length and breadth of my career, I could hand on heart say, "Nothing occurred on my watch" – that is, as far as I could reasonably tell. No one died on my watch.

That's not to say it doesn't happen on the least suspecting 'good' cops watch – it does; but I can say for me it didn't happen.

For all that time, though, you couldn't prove what you prevented. A frustrating and somewhat unfair conundrum, and dice with fate you are unwilling to play.

"Let's see what happens" – and someone dies as a result – is a stake too high to take as consequences become irreparable.

What you can get now, instead of good policing, is either a blame culture or 'too scared to make that call' type of decision. Or worse, over-policing.

Rather than justifying inaction.

Yet, make that call and decision any police constable should be competent and confident to make.

When I walked into custody sometimes with my prisoner not in handcuffs, I was made to justify why that was the case. A good search, active monitoring and engagement.

Those who routinely handcuffed, the justification was easier. I still query when I see peaceful protesters handcuffed on TV. Yes. Do stop cutting down our trees please. They breathe life and blossom. A police constable's automatic go-to response can be to 'over police', not to be that one it all goes terribly wrong for. But this is an inefficient use of resources.

"I must arrest you because we've had a complaint and my manager says so."

Blind authority is blind authority; however it starts out.

"I made that call."

"I told them to do it that way".

Those were the rarities of police speak in the corridors of retrospection.

There is no recognition or reward for all the hard work and toil that goes into prevention. The teams that win awards are those that respond and tidy up. Not the teams that work tirelessly, unseen the whole time.

I'm talking specifically about much of what went on behind closed doors. Peace isn't revered as much as it should be. Just don't say the 'Q' word for Quiet.

The intelligence departments, made largely of police staff and some restricted duties officers.

The CCTV unit, always prepared to view CCTV.

Anywhere.

Anytime.

For I alone could not have achieved much of what I felt I did achieve if it had not been for some of the hard working and diligent departments. I was quite often able to convince them time and time again to 'do that little bit more for me will you'. Bingo! Gotcha.

I've got enough now to escalate this properly, or solve the case.

So, when it came to an ordinary day in 2015, it was a football event and we were all sent to get some refreshments and grub whilst the match played. I saw the firearms officers and got into a conversation with them, which resulted in me joining them in their car to eat the rest of the meal I had got, to sit down with some colleagues as the lull of football play occurred.

I never worked with firearms officers, so we seemed to get

on all right. They're good with animals, the mentally ill, and me. It was a unit I never applied to go into owing mainly to lack of a) physical agility and fitness and b) worrying about the whole mental health history: as a young'un I had other ideas, though as I played with toy guns. As I enjoyed this meal, there I saw ahead of me hostile reconnaissance at play.

In hindsight, it was pretty brazen.

It was a bit obvious, but even the obvious works in plain sight reliant no one will do anything.

So I approached them.

They were secretly filming and it was a trap I walked straight up and into.

The video concludes with them throwing their rucksack to the floor. Clearly it didn't explode. I was getting nowhere with them to rule them out as a problem, or rule them out as a safe enough problem, as swiftly as you might expect any member of a civilised community playing games with you. You might expect them to rule themselves out as quickly as possible when approached by a police officer, when their behaviour has been overtly hitting all the reasons to go and speak to someone. Some attention seekers need ignoring. Not this one.

You'd think a member of any civilised community would want to help an officer rule them out of any investigation, so the true perpetrator can be found. Or the resource can go back to being utilised elsewhere. Or to give us a break and let us finish our grub one time.

Their whole objective, this occasion, had been to see if anyone would approach in the first place with the added bonus to set you up to look a bit silly.

No wonder I was confused by them.

I hadn't been prepared that someone was actually out there

to try make us look a bit daft. Naïve again.

No, they had another agenda in mind. The video they recorded would later be posted to social media for all to see. Of me.

Incorrectly marked up by them and labelled as 'unlawful arrest'

– which it was nothing of the sort.

Yet, still, there it was in black and white for all to see, and for some that was all they would need to see to cast their own aspersions of me as an officer.

How can something so inaccurate remain on the internet for years?

Any investigation I would OIC, someone could google me and assume I was incompetent on this written say-so. Where was their evidence of unlawful arrest?

Where was their evidence I had done anything other than my job that day? The feelings of being ashamed of that video, were all too vivid. This is because it wouldn't go away.

It appeared to be public property to laugh at police officers on duty by setting them up for pranks.

The bar and credentials on the evidence police officers are expected to prove for cases is so high. Often beyond reasonable doubt. The same cannot be said for some of the vitriol that can be spread about officers in turn.

Since then, I came to learn of a group who call themselves 'Incels'. I can't help but align the values of some of the comments I did go on to read as nothing more than salacious teenage boy comments, "PC BUTT FACE HAHAHAHA."

I'd still walk up to suspicious occurrences though, probably even now.

Although I had landed a little bit on my face there, it was a video that did taunt me.

Why was this new officer presenting me with a video of me? Who amongst my colleagues was talking about it, circulating it, sharing it, and laughing at it behind my back now?

Sometime later, I think it was over a year or two, the same individual would reappear at one of the big sporting events at Wembley.

This time, however, with a police 'entourage'.

Clearly for their own protection, as the sort of behaviour they got up to DID cause unnecessary bother. Generally, that bother was their idea of fun: to cause in others alarm and distress. To take away the resource of police that really should and ought to be spent on better things elsewhere. When they decided to 'unlawfully' record me for their own gain. I can say 'unlawful' right? It doesn't have to be true. Just like they could write 'unlawful arrest', it doesn't have to be true.

The law didn't always have a relevant bit of legislation to utilise, so sometimes you could get caught off guard until you could think on your feet just enough.

Disregarding entirely the magnitude of having walked up to them in the first place, rucksack adjourned, it wasn't until I read, as eloquently recorded, that action being one of the sole factors that might have changed the fate of Manchester's atrocity.

The firearms officers at my gig stayed in their car. Had I not been there, then who might have walked up to them and with what?

Sometimes people jump all over the police, but what is the alternative?

My attendance to that matter was recorded in the first

place. I am left now grateful for, as I look back. It wasn't the first hostile reconnaissance job I had stepped up to the plate to tackle. I had been trained in counter terrorism (CT). I didn't control-alt-delete what I learnt over the years because I switched departments. I took training and knowledge with me. I shared it on.

Even if it did become the same CT department I would be 'frogmarched' and kicked out of, – left rendered unemployed for a couple of month period in the police in 2009 before being reinstated.

That would be an interesting and unique experience once more. As a still accountant-minded soul, I took adversity to the over-ordering of buffet food and 'early' cutaway of police support staff. It was a hard lesson to learn that not one of the seconded surveillance officers, who's job I had made easier to reclaim their overtime, reached out to me in support.

It was my family who came to the rescue that time. I learnt the lesson then, there are a lot of takers from you in this life. Sometimes you need the givers.

I lost my home as I needed to rent it out, my job, and life almost – all for speaking up about inefficiencies and trying to do the right thing, again. I am not too sure whether, as a result of my own drunken arrest which coincided prior to that time, Mi5 had put a Xmas tree on my personnel file. My drunkenness was a liability, after all. I learnt how to become good at starting over again either way.

That department taught me a lot once again of credentials of an institution closing ranks, it taught me a lot about being a woman.

There had been this one-woman CT operative – who I always wondered how she managed deployments into hedges for months on end and her periods.

The first hostile recon job after this for me had been as mentioned in a reality TV show land. The programme had filmed in closed pubs, just for entertainment. I did my checks on much of what aired on the programme, and some of it was really only aired for viewers' entertainment purposes.

I was police staff that time and a special constable. I 'clocked' on, so to speak, when I should have been 'clocking off' as staff to see that CT job through.

I did what I thought was right.

So can you. You are that *one* in the community making the difference. Be the change you wish to see.

This account is written to say I tried. I did it. I joined the police service. I survived the police service, then I left the police service. I'm proud of this fact now, that I tried.

Had it not been for the very rich and diverse experiences it gave me I wouldn't have half the insight I feel I have grown to garner today.

This account draws parallels to other professionals out there. Any profession out there, actually. You hear it a lot. The institutionalised, the stayers. The sad losses of those who retire only to die within the first few months of 'freedom'.

Freedom from routine, stature, their identity.

When I initially failed my fitness push and pull test, but passed with help from others, it was a fit sergeant who helped me successfully pass a push and pull test, wanting nothing in return – when they retired, they passed away within months. I texted their phone on hearing the news, I couldn't believe it. My identity was wrapped up with the police, that's for sure. Almost impossible to separate. But it was a career that wasn't meant to be for the duration of my life. Like it can be for many others.

Some officers never return to their families.

I spent just shy of thirteen years in the police service. You used to be able to retire after twenty years. Then it moved to twenty-five. Then it moved to thirty. And finally, by the time I left, it had moved again to thirty-five.

That's thirty-five years to get the same pension, sort of, as those who had retired before, after twenty years. Different times. Or the consequence of inefficient times?

There is a human response to leaving any career, not just the police. That response can be grief, that response can be anger and sadness. Akin to any relationship severing, divorcing.

What went well:

A convicted paedophile, who's address I was sent to monitor, hid files within their computer cloud. I was able to detect their deceptive behaviour, to identify their continued offending habits.

That didn't go so well:

Rookie error: After arresting someone for being drunk and disorderly. In my statement, I wrote everything but the credentials for the offence. Namely, "Their eyes were glazed, their breath smelt of intoxicating liquor, and they were unsteady on their feet." I still wouldn't say it quite like that. So why would my statement say that? I would say, however, "They were drunk." That, however, is not enough.

Chapter 4
Anger

When George Floyd was murdered in America by an American cop, it reverberated across the pond by way of the Black Lives Matter (BLM) movement. By this time I was tube driving. The unions made up some 'BLM' badges. Before sticking the badge on. I did my research.

There is no point offering up support that can become short-lived and not meaningful just because everyone else seems to be following a growing movement. To offer meaningful support is to enact meaningful change indefinitely.

The BLM was a movement and one of its founding leaders was Patrice Cullors.

Patrice Cullors featured within a futurelearn.com course I did to better understand how I would explain my understanding of BLM, as a white person.

Of course, my initial reaction was to back this movement. But I am too aware of when the media can portray movements to achieve alternative objectives. In addition to this course, I got to learn about intersectionality. Intersectionality is a featured term coined by the scholar, Kimberle Crenshaw.

I implore you, head over and take these courses as there is nothing better than it coming from those incredible women's experience and knowledge. Gained via this free course opportunity. Whilst it remains remarkable and available.

Try courses. Personal development.

Kimberle Crenshaw, in particular, resonated with me. She had told of her accounts of being black and a woman in America.

She could join 'black' associations, or she could join 'women' associations – but there was no 'black women' associations.

It made it really clear to me how the intersections of what makes us 'us' interplays with the rest of the world around us.

Who could truly understand a black woman's experience, other than black women themselves?

When I say I support BLM, this is why I say it as one of the reasons. I can empathise, I can relate when it comes to intersectionality. Take, for example, my dyslexia and autism. These have been always present. This is an intersection of what makes me 'me' under the umbrella term 'disabled'. The conditions can become disabling. They shouldn't need be, in the right environment.

Kinder terms used are neurodiverse.

I am white. So I am privileged.

I am a 'woman' and that steads me for the same types of challenges any woman in this world may have to face from time to time.

Like Kimberle Crenshaw had explained through her experiences as a black woman. I could empathise with her experience because of my experiences as a now labelled-up disabled woman.

That's my understanding, at this stage.

The stark reality is that we, as women, can never really, truly be safe – at home, at work or anywhere – and is reverberated by the violence we may experience in every-day life.

When these intersections of what makes us 'us' interact with the world, and these interactions go badly, this can lead to a lot of unfulfilled potential. That may have gone differently, had it only been for a change in such intersections of what makes us 'us'. The unfulfilled potential works like an action potential. They cause friction, frustration, and anger. Anger can burst into power.

These aspects, these intersections of us, cannot be changed. So how do we reconcile? How do we thrive when the odds are stacked against us?

Along with all the other personal-defining intersectional characteristics.

Instead, shouldn't *we* be more preoccupied by what this person has got to say? What has this person got to offer the world that we all share a stake in?

When it comes to further misconduct in a public office. A documentary aired on BBC two, presented by Stacey Dooley called two daughters. The murders of sisters Bibaa Henry and Nicole Smallman.

The documentary described how murder scene photographs had been shared by two serving police officers, within a WhatsApp group containing forty individuals. One of the sister's friends remarks "when you send a picture to forty different people, you know those forty people think the way you think, have done that before, will be accepting of the behaviour – that came with those photographs".

Further reference is made to that being only the tip of the iceberg.

My experience of tackling WhatsApp's at work consists of a group of a dozen individuals within the police service. There began the belittling of our sergeant, body shaming them as they undertook a diet.

As I asked the group why they were saying and doing this, one by one like lemmings – individuals began dropping out of the group until it only consisted now of me and two. The WhatsApp work group no longer existed as it once did. It transpired later it did, it is just I was not invited into the new one. The new one got a rebranding as 'the raspberry dream team', no longer in fear of any reprisals or recriminations for their mutual appreciation to body-shaming behaviours.

A similar experience then occurred when as a tube driver, one of the drivers posts a suicidal person in distress on the tracks. Laughing between them at another's demise. Again, one by one, like lemmings people evaporate from the group, until it consists only of me, plus one or two. I asked the post be immediately deleted, is all.

One part of this misconduct story, that does not seem to be wider knowledge, is that it *must* have been reported. The crime scene photos had been shared within the group of forty. It otherwise would not have got out. For me, had I have worked in professional standards, I would have expected to have received thirty-eight emails, texts, voicemails. All reporting this same message.

I'd like to think optimistically this was the case, that the majority of the group did report it. Because what happens to those who don't do or say anything in protest? There are some cases, like this one where doing nothing should be treated as complicity to the crime. As an investigator, I would have held all forty individuals to account in some way – in the public interest.

What went well:

The Valentine's Day domestic: The sergeant walked into the office and said, "Does anyone want two jobs."

One of them involved CCTV capturing a lad holding a carving knife over a lass. It hadn't yet made it to the major crime team. They were seventeen-year-olds; I got it to the major crime team.

That didn't go so well:

Butter fingers: smoke had filled an office, nothing too serious, owing to smoker's butts outside catching alight. The room was self-locking. London Fire Brigade (LFB) arrived. When asking for access, I had to tell them I had dropped the only key inside the room as I left it and shut the fire door. They would need to do the heavy door in to gain access. After that, an emergency access key was erected on the wall outside the self-locking room. In remembrance of human incompetence and incapability to not drop a set of keys at the point they could be needed.

Chapter 5
Sadness

BLM is important to me because, aged eleven, I would experience what it was like to lose a friend. Years later now, I understand. It really is too late to say sorry sometimes.

Everyone is sad, sorry doesn't cut it.

After the road traffic collision that killed him, despite a week's medical intervention, the council erected a safer road sign and crossing. But an eleven-year-old black boy was killed there first. Why?

More often than not, you cannot prove what you prevent by being proactive in these matters. Everyone knew this stretch of road was dangerous, but no matter what the community might tell the authority about road safety, the reactive nature of many of the large organisations can be to react when they are meant to be seen to react. Akin to greenwashing mentality. Until that combustion point, things tick over.

It is why this black boy would have to die at age eleven from multiple trauma. I was reminded, on watching a documentary/drama about the telling of when eleven-year-old Rhys Jones shot and murdered on his way home from football practice, gunned down so innocently.

I vividly recall, on seeing the actor's eleven-year-old feet – as portrayed in the docu-drama – being touched by his parents, as all they could do for their son in that moment. Then me holding a pair of soccer socks of this late school friend once in my hand. An eleven-year-old sized pair, when held in an adult's hand, are so small.

We had returned from the end of a school year six abseiling trip to Wales, and I was tasked with handing out all the lost property back to the rest of the class.

This lad was the red soccer socks.

He loved football.

And I fancied his best mate.

I had crushed on this lad for years, his best mate, so it was inevitable, from their love of football, I too would acquire a love for a sport not meant for 'girls' at that time.

I became accustomed to wanting to know about football. To admit that, as a child, I had worked out that if I appeared to like soccer, then maybe that would make me appear more interesting to the boys. What a way to think.

This plan didn't work, like most of the best laid plans don't.

It's interesting, the reasoning and rationale of a child.

The propensity stays with you right through to adulthood (funny that) and well into adulthood, like a bad, lingering aroma.

This is where it has the capacity to really knock you off your stride a bit. The inner child can become stronger than the adult you have become.

Although children do come out with some *really* interesting observations from time to time, you wouldn't automatically go to them for advice on adult-related stuff.

Yet, this inner, childish dialogue can become default.

Why is it a lot of us get stuck listening to the advice of the remnants of the child part of us left inside? Why on earth would you listen to the wisdom of a child, as an adult?

The child part left inside you needs reassurance and patting on the back, that you're doing OK.

You need reassurance. You're doing OK on your own path. It doesn't need you as an adult to listen to that inner, insecure child and doubt your plans and self as an adult.

Not just the experience of an eleven-year-old child, but as far back as I can recall, being that four or five-year-old child left out of the playground simply because I hadn't bought 'fashionable' snacks in. Namely Walker's ready salted crisps.

I sat alone often in a library, or on the steps outside of the teacher's staff room, or with a coat over my head if forced to play out on the fields. Except, no one noticed or seemed to care for the sake or future of one child, when all the others were getting on fine in and amongst the crowd. It was a dinner lady who noticed I had stopped eating and reported that straight back home. What does the loss of one person's future mean? Usually the ripple effect is around twenty, or so I once read.

One person left behind, left out, excluded entirely from mainstream opportunities, makes for a crowd of lost opportunities.

The institution is only as solid and as strong as its individual parts.

Some parts are incomplete and need help.

So, how do we see more people you wouldn't usually see in positions they ought to be in? You let them in and let them stay. For me, the psychological trauma of being that round peg in a square hole was experienced as far back as that. Including the self-harm and suicide attempts. They didn't have a name for it then in the early 90s.

I guess, at some point, I parked this psychological fall-out away and carried on for a bit unscathed. But it would resurface in its abundance at that immediate moment that manager said:

"You're late."

My deep rooted, psychological, child-like response was to reply with the internal dialogue:

Alert! Hide! Take cover!

"You're not safe."

The rest of the autonomy for the nervous system kicks in then, fight or flight – the sympathetic nervous system kicks in. It doesn't switch off again. Not properly, it seems. Until you heal properly that is.

Battling mental health issues alongside an already demanding job, I think I did all right in the end. I could, of course, always have done better sometimes, depending on when hindsight came to call. Unfortunately, however, hindsight doesn't call ahead.

If only it did.

It would be a recording of me approaching a rucksack-carrying, attention-seeking social media aficionado, that I would have to contend with forever more. Yet now having resigned, I took back that video of me and owned it. As a means of getting over that unshakable feeling of feeling sad and ashamed of yourself.

I'm grateful there is record of me out there now, doing the job the best way I knew how to, at a point in time.

Taking a step forward sometimes, in the absence of any other takers. Even with a mouthful of food.

Some of the comments were positive as well. When I went back recently to where I was last shown the video, it appeared to have been deleted and reloaded, removing all traces of positivity and negativity. There is always hope of kindness materialising in the least expected places.

So, there lies my evidence, of my trying. Just for the wrong person, place, and period in time. Who would've known?

I'll take the part of me looking a bit silly for anyone, and for any stranger for that matter. We are all strangers until we converse in some way. The people who have helped me along my journey path, they were sometimes strangers to me.

I didn't get to know or see them all in person – but they were there, the whole time.

Sometimes it might have been a legacy they left for the world – proving to others the way to have better and brighter futures ahead of them.

A legacy is like a tree that faithfully drops its seeds below – in good faith, and not always knowing the outcome. My grandma donated her brain to medical research – she wouldn't be around for her conclusive results of suffering with dementia. Instead, she'd had a series of mini strokes. With advancements now in medical science, her contribution will have gone on to help many she would not be able to know of.

People like her, and many others, altruistically pave the way and give hope for others.

I hope this story acts as an aide to how I accomplished equilibrium again.

It's what worked for me, anyway. We are all different, but if even one ingredient that worked for me works for someone else, it could just be that 'missing link' or jigsaw piece needed to complete someone else's recovery.

Sometimes it is a lightbulb moment you need off someone else to lead to your lightbulb moment.

It is my intention that this prose may help you in some way, if not to at least understand an experience from another human being's perspective. If, like me, you are curious about others, that is.

When it comes to very human things that take place in life, including grief and loss. Especially when it occurs, like it can do, with any career change.

I try to keep everything as simple as possible as I go.

As for strangers, in 1997 it was the Arsenal team who signed a letter of condolences, which was read at our eleven-year-old's funeral. From then on, I knew football stars were legends.

Some with deep pockets, some with deep hearts.

It's something special when you reach out like that, to strangers.

Footballers can be that representative of a collective world and sport mentality and ethos. Of a spontaneous sense of belonging to something bigger. You don't have to fully understand it. But many of us die in the process of reaching Maslow's self-actualisation.

What went well:

A football fan left their wallet at home. So, I withdrew some cash, enough for them to continue their day out, without missing any of the match and going home for their wallet. They transferred the cash via bank transfer.

That didn't go so well:

Rookie error... who hasn't ended up on the wrong destination train? Well up North, I had found the public loos but got lost on the way back to the station. Had to ask locals for directions to the *police* station. I was in full uniform at the time and they thought I was joking.

Chapter 6
Depression

There will always be those individuals who 'hate' the police. It's usually either because they're doing something wrong themselves and don't want to stop it, be caught, and potentially punished for it.

Or they don't understand the police, not properly.

Ultimately, I have engaged in many conversations with police haters and asked them why they themselves haven't joined the police. To be the change they wish to see from within it. From the inside out. Usually their response is:

"I would never join the police."

I admire and respect their stand-point, I don't have to agree with it. I can hear them out. I can try to understand.

What is the solution? Hate doesn't solve anything. It makes it unpleasant, and worse. Since when has hate ever conquered love? It is love that conquers hate.

I headed to social media following the suicide of a prominent celebrity, who's work ethic I had come to know of and work incredibly close alongside.

I was and still am incredibly saddened by their high-profile suicide.

Sometimes, when you least expect it, something becomes a trigger that causes a catalogue or chain of events.

Conversely, this one triggered the dormant or 'depression' remission in me. A trigger isn't something to run scared from.

However, it is something that should be addressed, tackled head on when it arises. A trigger is your problem to deal with. You weren't born with it. Usually, it's something that happened to you that you need to find your own way to get over, put behind you, and move on from.

Depression, in me, was already present, lying dormant and untapped for a bit.

I resolved this turn of depression by starting a course of anti-depressants called Sertraline.

At the time I had read the news of this suicide, I was sleeping rough on a cold and dirty depot floor, as night tube had been halted owing to Covid-19.

I took a 'selfie' of where I was now compared with where I had been when my path had crossed with this celebrity a decade earlier. I didn't look great in the selfie. I didn't feel great and I was suffering from the effects of hypothermic conditions, lying and waiting sedentary to bring out the first trains that following morning.

A referral to occupational health later, they agreed a sleeping bag would be sufficient enough for me to return back to driving again. I didn't think walking around the underground with a sleeping bag would look professional. I didn't want any of our customers to start slipping me fivers, like they do for our resident beggars and buskers on board. It might have been an easy mistake to make.

This was yet another experience of what it is truly like to work for an organisation as large as TfL. You're a number again, just a number. There is very little regard given to you when you might need it, sadly.

So, again, it is you who has to triumph and find your way through against all odds.

Find my way through I did, but not before making some firm good friends in the process. Some enemies are also inevitable along the way. Especially when you challenge the way it is done.

This time I was angry, though, how can you not give someone any reasonable adjustments to level the plain.

This time it was meant to be different.

I resolved this depressive, potentially marriage ending precipitating episode through medication, exercise, podcasts, reading, learning, playing netball, brushing my teeth, eating well, and becoming more grateful. I would work towards achieving forgiveness.

What went well:

A man was reported to be strangling a woman. They both carried on with their journey. Painstakingly, I was able to trace the victim, which led to the identification of the offender.

That didn't go so well:

Rookie error… A late-night reveller in Town was ranting in my face. One of the police horses was giving me the eye. So, I looked at the more interesting horse, for a split second, as the ranting had got tiresome and boring. The late-night reveller noticed my loss in interest, which gave them a genuine reason to be annoyed. Forcing an apology. Which was enough for them to go on their way.

Side note: Strangling someone is deemed as a lesser offence, a common assault. Strangling someone should be treated as an attempted murder, that is how I treated it. The law can be an ass. You have to either lobby the government for years or be a somebody to get heard, for the law to be changed.

Chapter 7
Acceptance

When I could toddle, I toddled off out the house because, as far back as I could go, I was an 'alien' in the wrong place. I was leaving to find my 'right' place, a different planet to where I was.

No one could understand me. I didn't speak, and when I did, it was my own gibberish, which I perfectly understood.

On occasions, one of my brothers would interpret for me, I am not sure of the success of this because I simply do not remember it.

As soon as I was walking, talking, and sent to ballet, the social anxiety must have started.

Just like mice who have been given the anxious and autistic strain can do, I would begin to acquire a need for toilet urgency, when strained. Even wetting myself and occasionally pooping myself – which is semi-acceptable when you're a child. Not so much when you are a teenager, and least of all when you are a fully grown adult.

Yet this was my sympathetic nervous and coping system at play. At play for all the times I went misunderstood. For all the times I wasn't welcomed in, or included to be taught in a way I could understand. Often in remission, coping systems can kick start up again, at any time.

I now know, having studied British sign language, this comes down to methodology. For example, sign language is another form of communication. It is my belief that I may have had an alternative experience had I acquired this method of communication from an early age. Even if to say, "Hey! I need to pee, or poo."

So many people get left out because they are not considered properly.

Instead of this alternative form of communication, I would wet myself – usually in front of the rest of the ballet, singing, or school class, with children, peers, and teachers looking on in disgust.

Why can't this fully formed child 'toilet' like the rest?

There was one particular incident, when the most popular girl in my new school had started to like me, inviting me over to play even. A joy I could not express.

I returned this warm welcome to school by wetting myself right next to her. We were rehearsing a school play at the time, so it wasn't just in front of her, but the whole year group of, say, fifty-six kids.

I didn't come out the toilet for the shame afterward. The teacher had to call my mum to come collect me and coax me out of, aptly now, a very locked and probably quite blocked toilet.

This could have been the spot where social anxiety came out; you do your own timeline of events to reach back to the root cause of what might be causing you bother still to this day. The Speakman's regularly feature on ITV, I found this advice particularly useful.

The kids, teachers, and popular kid actually were all really good about it. When I allowed myself to remember it properly, it's me who was holding on to incorrect assumptions of how others perceived that incident.

Don't forget, when you rest your head each day, it is unlikely anyone is worrying too much about every nuance of your day like you are. They are all preoccupied worrying about their own days. Over time, guaranteed people can even forget you exist!

It's this type of bargaining that helps you reframe and reconsider what is holding you back. Bid yourself a better understanding of your own experiences and bid that others aren't all laughing at you, it is only the few that are too bored and invariably do, until they move onto the next least suspecting soul. You become old news.

I would pull a blinder on this popular kid. My once best friend. When they asked me, above all other credible and 'better' candidates, to be their maid of honour, it was like they had given *me* this honorary badge of excellence. I had made it to the 'top' and was someone's 'top' friend, above all others. Except I failed at the pressure.

I got rat-arsed at their hen do, then couldn't face the shame of standing in front of all their much better friends at the ceremony. I pulled out. I regret it to this day. Probably more than anything this. There is no bargaining to be had when you have let down your best mate, because you let down yourself.

This public wetting myself trauma was the porthole that got reopened again at the tune of that voice, "You're late."

You're not safe. You're in a world that doesn't get you. I only seem to have one picture of that class play on me these days. But it is a precious one. It has my eleven-year-old peer in it who died, and another kid who would go on to lose his leg between the train and platform interface as a young adult. He would become an amputee.

Now I would become a tube driver. How I feel responsible

for trying to prevent the next event like this. Only because I continue to see, hear, and feel everything that goes on around me and don't ignore the daft things that appear to be 'allowed' to take place. Just like the overdue invoices.

I do this by recording presently 'unrecorded' stats. People who touch the train but nothing happens *that* time.

At least it should be all our responsibility to show, at least, that we have considered others, and at least care to consider others.

I bother management when the occasion arises with these stats. It's the extent of my ability.

They forward it on to the health and safety team for review. Or so they say they do. If they don't know something is happening, they don't have to consider it. That is why I would always encourage people to speak to police, community groups, or organisations when something is affecting them. Saying nothing invariably leads to nothing being done. I always wonder how it is the case for those in positions where their influence could make the difference you need. Their influence and importance could be the factor that might change the outcome for at least one individual or soul. The ripple effect in not doing so can go on to reverberate through generations. The secondary victims, the family, friends, and society as a whole when systematic failures endeavour.

I always wonder how they don't use their power and influence more or wiser than just appearing in glossy pictures and media appeals when those events arise.

That's one of the saddest things I have come to learn of institutions. Something which I struggle to contend with to this day.

The front that is sometimes put on.

The reality that no one, at times, *really* cares.

So, when someone does die or becomes seriously harmed on a watch, it is partly an institutional responsibility for that. Or it should be. Individuals in influential positions could be held to account.

Especially if, when at the top, you are in an untouchable position where you don't need to let the small fry bother you any longer. You've reached the dizzy heights of power. You no longer look down or back from where you came from. If you even started down there in the first place.

The same place everyone comes from. Planet earth.

Take, for example, a news article where someone lost their life between the train and platform interface at Waterloo Station in 2020.

Conversely, I had a meeting with some senior people shortly after that time. Totally unrelated to that event and after that date. I would never have told by their demeanour that they had just had a death occur in their jurisdiction and watch. A key finding of the report, is that there doesn't seem to be in existence a continual dynamic risk assessment.

Yet here was I, identifying yet another anomaly in the system and wanting to do something about it proactively.

Nothing is spoken about like this at work. Not this. Not what went well or could've gone better. From my CIMA accounting days, I took this from that life-long learning. But it appears to be unique only to accounting. Not public service.

There was one occasion where I came to take note of the use of force necessary to successfully manage an individual. If touched they would enter into an extreme psychological reaction. Drawing parallels to how the police can manage public order situations, it was clear if training and awareness could be shared then they too could be successfully managed – without an officer having to touch them, or minimally invasively. I emailed the training school and asked about them using this as a case study, that it was for the interests of everyone to continually be mindful of adapting their working style to suit their audience. Driven again by my experiences from the night time economy, it echoed conversations I had held with licensees about how door staff managed drunk patrons. No one wants door staff or police arrested for unnecessary use of force. Intoxicated or in mental distress? Verbal direction can be as effective as any physical means of force, as hearing is often the last sense to leave us, when incapacitated.

'Every contact counts' is a phrase I learnt that is also true from that time. Every contact does really count. It should leave a trace that is impermeable.

The 'Untouchables' are those that don't do anything and are OK with that. The 'Touchables' are those statistics that it eventually happens to and have no choice as to be OK or not with it. Their only choice is to learn to live with it or die trying.

The front-line bottom of the rank, left to sweep up when the system goes cataclysmically wrong and a catalogue of errors or unrecorded statistics ensue.

Even when the front-line is telling those in positions who can do anything about it how to prevent the next one. Still, it is the expectation that the front-line will deal with it anyway when it does happen, AND still be held to account for the next one, and the next one, and the next one.

Even though the cogs in the wheel could have been turned or influenced differently earlier, coming from higher up the chain down before that point. If there had been willingness for it, to take up prevention opportunities up until that point.

Accidents or incidents happen as a result of many 'mishaps', or a catalogue of errors or omissions.

I will always endeavour to be that cog in the wheel, where it is possible for me to intervene. My way is by recording these stats and sending them on, even though I really don't have to.

No one is asking for them and they could be made easier to report.

If the inevitable then happens on my watch, so to speak, I know the process of dealing with that will be possible for me to achieve and let go of.

I will be able to say, hand on heart, "What else could I have done?"

A form of forgiveness and bargaining one does with their own conscience and soul. If you're on a train and you hear an unusual but informative announcement about safety, it is my way of giving the public the information – information they have free will to do what they will with.

This comes back to Marcus Rashford's Gran's analogy of what you have control over. The inner circle; I have control of. The outer circle – a.k.a other's – I do not. Read *his* books.

Returning to football, this other peer of mine, they would go on to captain England's amputee team. Their social media video is inspirational, but so is their apparent struggle.

In the video, they profess they wish they had known about amputee soccer sooner. To join this soccer team. I can only otherwise imagine such a recovery to be isolating and debilitating, yet there existed the England Amputee Football Association (EAFA).

I kind of imagine netball being the equivalent tonic. I joined a netball team in Kidbrooke, South London, even though unrelated to my area. It was where there was opportunity to reconnect, re-join, and be part of something regularly playing together. Joining and reconnecting with a team sports like this aided my recovery from depression. It was a case of trial and error, bargaining what works and fits now in this whole new world. Community really is a panacea. Accepting all the parts that contribute towards completing you.

Alongside the course of anti-depressants, Sertraline, I had watched Roman Kemp's 'Our silent emergency' BBC Three documentary that had featured his friend's suicide on it. There he kindly shared he had been on Sertraline for much of his adolescent and adult life. This was remarkable to see. Such a prominent and successful individual saying, "I am medicated to be me and thrive."

"It's OK". It's OK is a useful phrase to follow any negative thought pattern with. "But it's OK". Delete that negative programme.

My autism and dyslexia reports had suggested medication, the touch of ADHD, hyperactivity, and insomnia bouts is typical to autism. My baseline default position is pretty happy.

So, when this recent work anomoly arose, where they simply 'forgot' my reasonable adjustments for dyslexia as one example,

I took to re-read what all these experts had said about me once. That was part of the cracking of the enigma code, let's revisit what makes me 'me' from others' perspectives.

I knew what I needed. I had relayed it to my new employer, but the attitude I mostly experienced was anyone can tube drive. Perhaps that was anyone before me; I don't wing things. Medication kept me employed there until I became experienced enough.

As for netball, there is a presently underused netball courts often overlooked by hospitals in local parks and green spaces. The potential for rehabilitation is huge and I am working on that. I have visions and goals to work towards achieving, outside of the police. It comes down to that 'one bad day' incidence that can have the propensity to lead you down the path of 'it's a whole bad life' attitude and the subsequent self-fulfilling prophecy that then ensues.

It's psychological warfare, and yet you are the 'warrior' and 'persecutor' of yourself. In other words, we can be our own worst enemies. As much as we can be our own best saviours. It might explain why suicide can be pervasive.

One thing I have learned recently is to be really in tune with what my mind and body is telling me it needs. Be it sleep, be it food, be it company, be it education. Serve it.

When I began to experience pain all over my body, I realised it was because I was not listening properly to it. I was not waking it up with its cup of tea, namely exercise, like I do to brighten my mind in the morning sunrise. Or sunset, depending what shift time I am on.

It was a recent set of counselling I had that got me to reconciliate this imbalance.

"You and you alone are the only person in this world that has to be comfortable in your company the whole time, twenty-four-seven, no one else does."

It does much for your expectations of others. There comes a point when you have to accept your expectations may need re-evaluating.

And with that, in combination with a mass purchase of self-help books, I began the arduous process of piecing back together, to amelioration towards the latter stages of grief, and life after the police. Acceptance. Acceptance of my current sit rep.

I won't tell you all the self-help books you need to read. But start reading or listening more in short. Acceptance will come. Forgiveness will enable you to finally, let go.

Amongst the self-help books, I always chucked in a few spins of the wheels or 'lucky dips', mostly by randomers I had never heard of. Just for fun, variety, and surprise.

Namely, I liked the front cover or something hooked me about a topic I had previously little to no experience of. Like medicine. I then went on to complete a neuroscience and psychology post graduate certificate.

Maybe this read, too, was a lucky dip, or punt of goodwill and support towards another human being's story, and you find yourself reading it. To garner understanding for another or yourself. Perhaps you will now join the police in some capacity on the back of it. Do. Be strong. Stand your ground. I managed thirteen years-worth.

Recalling that we are suspicious of what we are not familiar with – or we dislike the uncomfortable feeling of the unknown.

Part of my tonic, my remedy to fixing me, was becoming comfortable with the uncomfortable; me.

It's interesting I am a bookworm now. There was a time when the only book I had read cover to cover was Roald Dahl's fantastic Mr Fox. I could never tire of the cunning fox's circumvention of the cruel tactics to root out their family's den in the first place. That or the story of digestion, from grape to conclusion.

To Kill A Mocking Bird was a GCSE examination book, and even that I didn't bother to read properly. Instead, I picked one chapter, wrote some ideas about it, and low and behold got lucky that some of those ideas came to fruition by way of a question on it. Now I read books, word for word, and sometimes make notes. People do change where change is needed.

An A* I would achieve for that English Literature module was the only A* for the only subject I didn't focus much on. I nailed it. Somehow. I would go on to excel in other matters like this, like achieving a first in a time written assessment at university. Sometimes it comes down to hitting the structure right, and having a good day to boot. Getting the right combination to spin all at the same time.

The books I seem to read nowadays seem to be written by doctors, they stimulate my curiosity for life and learning from it. It is a shame in order to reach any PhD myself, I would need to conquer academic writing. Until academic writing is made less rigid, I'm happy to stay with my title of 'Miss', 'Mrs 'or 'Ms'. Ma'am is reserved for Inspector's and above.

I'm not the best writer or speaker, but I'm enjoying it more and more as I go along. Dyslexia? What?

Elements of feeling lucky has always featured in my life.

I had no idea there were 'ghost writers' out there. Until now. That is, people who write the books for other people.

I thought, this is a bit of a cheat isn't it. They decree themselves as 'authors', yet someone else wrote it for them. I hadn't realised it was the same with stand-up comedians, some of whom write their scripts, with whole teams behind them.

Where is the actual author's credit?

They are just telling the story for you

so that others are interested enough to read or hear it. But it's a front, is it not? Fronts don't appear well once scratched a few layers beneath the surface. In my creative work post police,

I don't plan to make a penny from it. Although I have had to spend a penny. I sometimes imagine, if money was taken out of most of the equations, how different collective life may be. How much more might be achieved if people sometimes did things for others for nothing materially in return. I won't be heading to the money-less commune anytime soon. They do, however, live an interesting life. Everyone has a role; everyone has a position and place to fill.

When it comes back to putting together all the ingredients, for a good day to happen and therefore good life on reflection, the mind is structured well enough to communicate those thoughts eloquently enough. When it wants to. Brain plasticity is something I am working to recover. I think it's working out OK. OK is enough sometimes. It's OK.

To combat insomnia bouts, I have learned my tonic is to tell my brain I am tired. And I seem to fall asleep. Podcasts helped with that 'lightbulb' moment.

I was introduced to podcasts by a colleague who was pregnant and inspirationally working very public facing at Victoria station. What a lot of podcast choice there is out there to behold. There is something for everyone. Just like there are books. Read books. Listen to podcasts. Find your tonic. Find your lightbulb moment and then enjoy the presence of time in the here and now – you've got the time to invest in you.

As for pregnancy, it seems to be contagious. A baby would spontaneously come along for me, a sweet spirit and soul who wanted to get to know me as a mother. My ex-husband on the other hand did not want to know me as a mother. The choice was made to turn over a new page yet again, into the next chapter of this new life, alone.

Alone, yet with the backing of a community, a whole Island

this time, an Isle of Wight family who welcomed us both, me and this Caulkhead native Islander now. They say it takes a village.. and for me, a wickedly awesome step-mum as a birthing partner.

What went well:
Trafficked child: A child was begging but refused to give their correct age. I was able to point out their trainers were children's; which led them to be taken under social care control.

That didn't go so well:
We were doing a revenue operation, but I urgently needed the toilet. My deposit blocked the station toilet, as the flush couldn't handle it. I had to find the cleaner's bucket to give it the nudge it needed along its way. We rounded up the revenue operation pretty quickly after that and vowed between us to not return for a while, so station staff might forget us.

Chapter 8
The Last Job

My attitude. Much of my regret and guilt lies in my attitude. Part of my accomplishments in the police was the strong sense of right and wrong I felt.

I would go as far as to say I even despised, or thought I would despise, those police officers who ended up getting sacked for one thing or another. Hate is too strong a word.

I would often read the independent office of police conduct IOPC reports; namely to see case studies and learn from other officers' mistakes or omissions, so as to try not to repeat them.

I listened well in training. I heard the grieving family accounts of members of the family surviving those who had died, not just at the hands of the assailant but because police had not quite done their job well enough in the nick of time.

I became well-rehearsed in my job as a result.

I practiced it and practiced it well.

To the point where I could reliably and consistently spot rookie mistakes or experienced senior officers missing the massive glaring red flag warnings within a job's credentials as they allocated out crimes for investigation.

More often than not, I would bid to repair them.

I would never ignore them for someone else's downfall. You would think this would be an invaluable asset to hold.

It was to a certain extent because it gave me more experiences.

Experience breathes confidence.

Instead, however, when I asked to be able to do what was required, this was for a different matter within my capacity within the system.

It became apparent, in order to do whatever was required, sacrifices would need be made. I would need to sacrifice myself to the point of burn out on some occasions.

Go it alone. No team buy-in. Or being bottom of the pile, managing without work attrition resources; for example, differing service level agreements. Major crime team would get everything same day almost, if you're bog standard response or neighbourhood, you are waiting in queue far longer.

Team buy-ins consisted of team haunts.

I'd do the work required, miss out on the team building, and inevitably burn out or be excluded.

I would be seen again as the odd one out, the one to watch, not in a good way, but to be suspicious of. I had sick leave a couple of times during my career, and I was left to feel guilty and ashamed of it when instead I may have benefitted from compassion and kindness. Which was achieved when working with medical professionals in the main.

I remember when it came to acting professionally, there was this one occasion a lorry of chickens had overturned. We, the police professionals, were called to assist with road recovery as all these wayward chickens who were living their best life all over the middle of the highway. Doing what chickens do best, and crossing the road. As a result, it was causing traffic jams.

Firstly, my vegetarian self was encouraging towards all these chickens and their great escape, but, secondly, I had never known how you professionally 'hold' or even catch a chicken in my life. Despite being a farmer's granddaughter.

One of the skippers appeared to be a natural at this.

They were like an animal-loving Dr Doolittle, scooping the feral winged birds one after the other, like a true police professional would. Back into these crate-like contraptions one by one they went.

"How and where do you learn to pick up a chicken like that, Sarge?"

I think in the end I left them to that and updated the drivers stuck in the traffic that it wouldn't be too much longer now, until traffic was moving again. Queue management was something I relished in. I would bid to keep everyone informed. It comes down to managing expectations.

When I had taken some sick leave, as a result of burn out – it was because I wanted to keep the club open, it was on my own head, and mental health be it. I achieved that for sure. At around the same time, someone senior had decided they were going to be amalgamating three licensing roles into two anyway, and joining area jurisdictions together.

As the three of us licensing officers got pushed to work together, one of them would touch my arse whilst getting into the motor on route to a meeting to discuss our regions, and the other one would leave my out of office voicemail on as follows:

"SHE IS OFF SICK."

And they were spitting feathers as they took over my voicemail.

Nothing professional or courteous about it but, in their view, I guess there was nothing professional or courteous about becoming sick either. They had survived the indiscriminate physicality of cancer and worked through it. Mental health relapses aren't seen on par equivocally to cancer.

Despite many similarities and risks to life associated in

both. Nobody asks for either. It can be indiscriminate.

Taking any sick leave is a bad idea, especially if you think you might escape or avoid something you would be better off facing sooner. It might, however, take sick leave to get there. But, for now, the sooner the return the better.

When it came to point scoring out that third licensing officer for the chop, it was apparent I wouldn't score enough points to be left included, owing to less service in and sick leave.

This is where the concept of leaving or retirement became a credible option for me anyway.

For some, retirement wasn't a credible option. I've made retirement a credible option 'now' – where I explore and try and achieve things I couldn't usually achieve whilst 'in the job'. Retirement is not best served left just for retirement. You can retire in your own style.

The licensing officer who scored the most points had been in the longest. Around forty years. I wouldn't want anyone pushed out of any post, especially because of age – but here lay an experience where the system allowed individuals to go up against each other and be scored, leading ultimately to the demise of one over another.

The whole process seemed cruel. Conversely, I couldn't make myself any older, to have been in service any longer than the other two. Sick leave aside. The sick leave therefore became irrelevant.

Age discrimination doesn't affect one end of the scale, it affects everyone on the scale, if the right context amounts as it did here.

I was too young to survive to keep my bum in that seat, but equally I had been on the lookout for change anyway, and I was ready for it. Being ready for change means to expect some.

In my family of self-employed workers, they are working well into their seventies and eighties because they love what they do. I guess those still working well into these ages in the institutions must love what they do, because they choose to still be doing it.

Or is it because, as I have outlined in this account, work actually becomes your identity, and a form of relationship in which would mean that, if you have to leave, you would have to sever some part of yourself. You would ultimately have to lose part of you and inevitably grieve for that loss. A bit like a divorce. I really can sympathise with the generation millennials, X, Y, or Zees – because the system is set up so that everyone is having to work longer to reach their pension. The excuse we are all living longer, I don't entirely buy.

I recall a lad recently, no more than twenty years old, crying at one of the ticket machines at work. When I went to see if he was OK, he told me he had spent all his money already, topping up several times that week on his commute.

What could he do to get to and from work?

There was I, a tube driver, albeit a part time one, with free travel for both me and a plus one resident living at my address.

Perks of the job, entitlements of a job, yet here was the evidence of proof for a whole generation of individuals being left out.

One group benefitting over another – where is the group objective and success in that? Why am I now succeeding yet others remain left behind?

Do I need my plus one oyster? Do I even need my oyster, on my generous salary really? This kid did. I wish I had told him to recruit into our world. If you can't beat them, join them?

I wasn't *that* helpful in the end.

All I did was apologise to him, that I couldn't help him.

I didn't help him. I could have given him some more options or food for thought maybe – but that was only with retrospective thought. He was long gone by that point.

He wasn't crying any more, though, because I had snapped him out of his immediate quandary.

To get himself home, he would need to withdraw, top up, and pay the system some more cash. Which he decided was his best and only option to do.

The system is one of the reasons why I came out of the tube pension. The evidence of another inefficient system, driving you to work for thirty-five years. That's why the six-month delay in starting with BTP, and the additional five-year pension goal post, didn't matter to me.

One thing is certain, I will retire, as I have done, in my own way, under my own steam, when it is suitable to me. Not when the system dictates it to me.

Recently at work, a colleague was going through how much the deductions were in the last few years leading to his retirement. It's some cruel game that, to keep people actively in when they might be otherwise ready to leave. They call it 'the golden handshake'. I call it 'the golden handcuffs'. My retirement, I look forward to a frozen police pension, which will give me an additional five to six hundred pounds a month when I reach that relevant retirement age goal. If, of course, I make it that long into this life. I know where home is – home can be made anywhere. That pension amount of money should be sufficient enough.

I am already sort of retired in my head. I am doing what I want to achieve now.

Imagine someone passes you a post-it note. The post-it note reads:

"You only have today to live; what are you going to get done?"

That's one way to prioritise. That's one way to appreciate everything you *have* got.

I am dipping in and out of things I have always wanted to do.

The job I do currently isn't for life, I get that – now. It's a blooming well-paid job for now. But I don't and can't expect to stay in it forever. It comes back to that institutional notion of the stayers; too scared to enact change and do something else for a bit.

It's those who remain well-rooted in positions, and you have yet more younger people either out of work, or unable to move on in positions in life – like getting their first home.

When someone is really that comfortable and safe in their job, they have no reason to give it up – of course. Why should they consider all those who might benefit from their leaving and vacating that position as swiftly and as efficiently as we all perhaps could alternatively work towards?

I'm in work for as long as my need dictates. Once I don't need to be there any longer, I probably won't be.

I'd have been moved on anyway, at least by an ever-changing system, is what I have come to expect anyway. Driverless trains, probably. The inability to strike any longer, probably. Not that I would strike. Having left the unions fairly early on, after joining them albeit briefly. Once again, to know someone or something, sometimes you have to join them.

One thing in life is certain; change. Change is always coming.

So, be prepared to adapt and thrive in it. I remember knowing, really knowing people, when I saw that licensing officer of about two careers worth hold so tight to their post they would see a twenty-something female ousted instead. There was some form of social cruelty in that, somewhere. Or at least I saw it that way, for what it was.

Conversely, if I had gone for the jugular of the other licensing officer who had shoved me into the car by my arse, they perhaps wouldn't have even been in the running for that much-sought-after second position either. But just like when my hair had been pulled by that councillor, I didn't see it as an assault back then. I didn't want to cause a fuss – perhaps at the points when it really should have mattered to cause a fuss – and scene in the name of self-preservation. I should have been a bit louder, or tactical.

All I could think in the rat run for those two-out-of-three positions was what are you really fighting for in the end? To do the work of at least three people into two people as the system now dictates it to be done – there was more than enough in my jurisdiction alone for three people to do, let alone to take on the work of two other areas with it. That was the job where I spun plates.

It's fine, you both continue to manage on. You can keep those jobs. Because I am embracing this change and challenge – and I am getting myself another job anyway. That's when I was accepted into BTP and was waiting to start.

That's when I spent the last six months working my time out in the domestic abuse office. Despite murders having taken place, the piles of risk assessments still mounted up. I couldn't sense any urgency amongst the team to reach this pile either.

Especially when one of the team had their own wedding to

plan. Which seemed to be their only priority. That is where 'they will get you out' was spat, with feathers along to boot. Get you out, maybe, but what am I really getting out and away from in the first place, if that be the case? I would know more about that by 2019. When I left the police service.

When it came to the death of the nightclub, it was when the neighbourhood inspector, without consulting police staff me, said yes straight up to one of the feeder bars going until two a.m. Although, as police staff, there was no place within the rank and file – professional courtesy would be to at least be seen to liaise with, rather than be seen to be the 'decision maker'. Their decision, as it was recorded, opened the flood gates to everywhere else applying, and in my own mind, contributed towards the death of the nightclub scene. There is great spirit to be found amongst a congregation of people.

There could have always been that linear separation; the nightclub being the only venue you could go to – to dance your night away until the small hours – and the bar to reacquaint with old friends before the club. Change was coming for everyone. Greed was the monopoly that saw already successful bars want even more – and to take from others.

The nightclub would have to change to adapt and thrive once more. Except, all these other premises wanted part of their slice – and now they were being granted it carte blanche. What could I do but agree to their application? The inspector had said 'yes' in a minuted meeting, you try work back from that. Minutes of which I was the minute-taker for as well. My remit is everything, remember. I really did do a good job to manage all that one job meant for three in the end – and one thing is certain, there is always an end.

Towards the end of that post, I wasn't able to handle as

much any more. I recall spending hours with a licensee, typical as I would when catering to an individual's need. They ended up spending hours lying to my face in the end. Their party went off, and the neighbours complained again – as was to be expected when giving the police duff information.

Although I knew the sense of right and wrong, because I always felt 'wronged' whilst trying to get on and do jobs, this portrayed a lot in my behaviour, and I often found myself frustrated and angry. So, colleagues invariably found me rude. Especially when they weren't doing their job properly. I was trying to get to the point of what I needed, but no one could interpret me again. Least of all help me out a bit by doing their job properly as well. No fun either way to be around.

You want to keep that nightclub open. You're on your own there. Disease was really eating away at me and my credibility again. The licensee who spent hours lying to me – they got a written warning, but it certainly wasn't anything I was proud to be the author of.

It was my turn to start spitting feathers. When you give people every opportunity and they piss all over it, it gets at you eventually. There really is nothing else I can do now – all of you, you're really on your own. Good luck, I'm gone.

Knowing when to give up is an important feature of being able to help others as well as yourself. Yet, it was one of these experiences where I saw who's side Occupational health was on. On one occasion, they would disclose to me an email they had received about me that simply read that, in the opinion of the sergeant, I wasn't mentally capable of doing the job. They added that they needed them on board with this. This wasn't how they had come across to my face. I'd be more capable with just four jobs, like everyone else, if that's what they were getting at. Their words were unkind. I guess the sergeant was saying that I, as part of the community, am mentally incapable of being in *this* community. For we are all mentally sound, right?

The NHS always helped me out, be it A&E or the community mental health services. How they did so was a marvel because it seemed to come to them so easy, what I needed. To be heard.

Russell Brand has a phrase in his book, Mentors, that says, "Greatness looks like madness until it finds its context."

I was always set to be a bit of a mad one in the police, as I wasn't always surrounded by like-minded individuals. I strived to deliver. The insidious environment bred insidiousness. But I knew my friends in the process, and they remain my friends outside the police also. When one of them left the police and resigned, they went travelling the world. I joined them in both Vietnam and Canada – they were thriving once again. Or the retired ex-colleague who went on to have a baby. They are just tired all over again.

Occupational health were always on my side and team.

They saved me many a time when no one else would, could, or wanted to save me. Most of the times I survived were because one or two excellent officers or staff came along at just the right and critical tipping point. They would become mentors and friends inevitably as well.

I guess I hope I was that 'one' person for others, too, at points.

Remember, in a rank and file organisation, you do not query up. For in order to do so, you will set yourself apart as different, non-conformist, and trouble.

It's absurd to me to not want to spend your own time with

colleagues-turned-friends So for my thirtieth I put on a lavish party for all my police colleagues to attend. I hired a venue and one hundred people accepted. I catered accordingly. On the night a dozen turned up. The place was empty, but it was filled with love anyway.

Instead, colleagues would only have meals together and insist on it whilst together at work.

Paid to work, paid to socialise together.

Paid to poo, that I could agree to.

Especially a bank holiday double-pay poo.

Double-bubble.

Otherwise, when I was at work, I was there to deal with any job at hand.

That brings me to my last job I dealt with. It had started two weeks earlier, in fact. I was told to look at a job and call the informant back.

"I'm not calling the informant back, I know them."

And this is why. Experience.

The original call had been an immediate call for service to look for a suicidal person. The response crew had rushed out, sergeant to boot, and sped through the narrow streets of London to arrive at the location. Except there was no one to be found. They did a bit of an area search, asked staff if they had seen one person in a million pass through the station. That was even a step more than a usual blue light crew.

The response crew then got to drive away, having done the 'fun' blue light response call.

A blue light call and run I would never be allowed to do myself, unless as the car sick passenger, because I had asked for some help, when it came to preparing for the course and theory test. I like to do things properly. I don't like to fail if I can help it.

Although failure has its uses. That was much of what guilt I held for leaving the police. That I never became a response driver.

Surely the epitome of what makes an officer is their response 'nee naw' car. I always felt kicked in the stomach a bit when every new officer after me was seemingly getting this course, and I now was not.

Goal posts moved.

"You now need to be a basic driver for six months. But you're also on restrictions, so now you are not even eligible."

Had I have got it, I promised myself I wouldn't take the tube driving role. I would've continued on regardless. With a new lease of life.

Drag racing through the night shifts, colleagues who did get the courses always seemed to spend them badly.

Of course, I would tell on them. I was jealous. Why were these miscreants all getting courses, driving like maniacs, yet I was not eligible? I disclosed my mental health, what does it say for their mental health to always be exhilarating seeking?

I was angry, I was depressed, I was excluded again. So, I taught my ex-husband and offered others lessons on how to drive instead. He passed first time and only on ten lessons, like me. I became a teacher and mentor in my own way.

He's pretty terrible when it comes to parking contraventions and regularly fined, I did however give him the choice whether to considerately park or not. Get ignored. Get over it. Better still, get a divorce! Always listen to your inner voice and gut instinct when it comes to people.

As for the blue light response accreditation - I guess I got over it.

I would never brake so hard to get a prisoner to fly forward in the crate, as I too had sat in the crate at one point in my life – and it remains an eligible position any one of us can land in. It was still happening over ten years later this practice; bad policing all around me.

And me as a constant witness to all of it for what felt like most of the time.

I didn't ask to be put in that position; it happened that way.

It was tiring. All the while I was made to feel like the inadequate cop who wouldn't get the response driving course, or any course now for that matter.

I was socially inadequate, was my crime, not community illiterate. Job after job I worked on, I worked on well. I made connections that lasted and had meaningful encounters, until that position was made redundant or I was told to move on from it. I even recall speeding to a job on foot towards Charing cross, it was six-thirty a.m. and I was in the locker room preparing for my seven-a.m. start.

I decided to try take a bus and then on foot but still arrived after the first initial responding unit had. They had booked on by seven a.m.

So, I got to scene preserve and stand on the entrance and exit, guiding members of the public as the station was now closed.

Got papped in the process, so there is evidence of that. I did not get to be first on scene or deal with the subject there.

But I had no other means of getting there.

I still tried, despite every barrier the establishment put up for me. I tried to circumvent or navigate around it, if I could. I just never could run fast enough to outrun a police driver on response. But I still tried. It was London after all!

When I refer to my last job, I'm really glad I did try to resolve it the way I did. I was leaving anyway, right?

It turned out to be the epitome of what many police jobs potentially could be and that was to become a complete and utter cluster-fuck.

The prison service or courts or probation had meant to circulate the subject as wanted, as they had not kept up with their probation terms. Again.

However, they hadn't done this six months earlier when they should have done – as a result, the subject had carte blanche been left out to fend for themselves again.

No wonder they may be feeling a little suicidal. Any form of rough sleeping is enough to push anyone over the edge. Or to self-medicate or do drugs. Except this time I had learned one of their loved ones, their support network, had died. Enough to push anyone to suicidal ideas. It was a sad set of affairs, this person. It was a life lost to addiction,

turned street life, and with the inevitable knock-on effect on their loved ones, friends, and family.

The regulation of narcotics and drugs could turn this form of deleterious existence to extinction.

The legalisation of drugs can already be found if you look around you a little more closely. Anyone with a bit of spare cash seems to get up to it these days, except they manage to function in both work and with their habits on the side, you would never know one from the other. Like some forms of alcoholism.

I know of serious sounding professionals smoking heroin or doing lines at the weekend, or on campus – except they don't have the stigma of homelessness or unemployment to interfere with their so-called recreational use habits. They have enough social standing for their habits to be acceptably received and go mainly unchallenged. Conversely, some of the more apt criminals, hide behind professional fronts too. You see begging on the trains and streets, yet they become the first people to get picked upon for when some of them go on to smoke their crack or shit in the door ways more blatantly than the office worker might. They at least can do it in their office block toilets unseen, unregulated.

The infrequent flyers aren't the ones that get caught up in the system of illegal drug use.

It's the last job I did which epitomises how wrong we are handling drug laws in this country.

That we could and should be modelling our addiction treatment on countries who already have legalised forms of drug administration, so that souls at least have the option to integrate back into society, to work, to live, and to coexist other than on the curt ledges of the streets. Maybe even like alcoholism, give it up in time – with the right support and context around them.

The government might save a bob or two. As well as make a bob or two.

The desolate deserve the same opportunities as those who were bought up with enough cash to choose to go and do it.

In taking a turn down the legalisation route, this could, in turn, reduce knife crime and the gang culture that goes on. Bankroll the system to be the drug administrator. I am so surprised it has yet to be seen as a money-making endeavour by the authorities.

Who, I quote, will go out to tender, or consultation, as to how as an organisation 'we' can make changes and or savings.

I replied to one such as this with, "Have you thought how you could make money instead?"

I think a personal assistant replied with a date and time to join in the discussions, rather than post it to the forum in which they had asked for feedback, albeit rhetorically. They already know who the next cull of posts will be. Consultation is because they legally have to be seen to be consulting.

Why don't they bid to remove the illegality from the streets? Drugs is both a health and crime matter, it is a societal issue and it is epidemiological at its function. Unless the status quo is all we can strive for?

When I attended this last job, on discovering this new information, that one of their loved ones back home had died, we had to find them. I wouldn't have got further information from the informant, it would have wasted time, when I knew who else would be a priority contact to establish a reliable sit rep with instead. It was beyond rare to decide 'not' to contact someone. Or 'not' do something considered 'usual practice'. So, on discovering this new info, we had to know how they were coping with this significant change now. A welfare check was the priority – but no one was doing one. Even if that would mean arresting them for the breach-turned-warrant and bringing them back into the fold of the system and process again.

We can at least conduct a suitable and thorough welfare check on them. It isn't great for them, they might have to go 'cold turkey', but there is always a means to an end to getting fed within the system.

You get to know people quite well whilst awaiting the custody checking in process. If the officers engage with them enough.

One beggar told me they made three hundred pounds a typical day, much more than me. There was satisfaction in their telling me this, as I stood there within the custody queue, attending their every need whilst all the while going hungry, thirsty, and in need of a toilet break no doubt myself.

Owing to the restrictions I had been placed on prior to this last job arising, and for reasons not explained to me then at the time. I was left to sit and rot on a broken chair in the end – the end date was now in sight. It was a waiting game.

Part of me thought they had restricted me because they thought I might do something crazy, mad, and stupid, like you sometimes read in the newspapers or hear on the news when people act out a course of revenge. The Dunblane shooter apparently wrote to the late Queen, but it seems the information was not triaged effectively to prevent it. He therefore went unheard again and acted out his course of anomie. That's how little they understood. I understood even less how they were able to restrict me. Just because of rank and file.

In the end, they misused a health and safety matter apparently. Occupational health would have agreed, like always, I'm fit and well and better to be operationally policing rather than restricted. The faceless senior officer deciding my fate had found some health and safety point to restrict me over. I think I had complained of weight gain and so they went down the unsympathetic nervous system was going to kill me owing to the stress. *They*, the 'rank and file', were the cause of my stress, not the job itself. This was so abundantly clear to me every time I had to go through the healing process of explaining why I was in the midst of what seemed to be another mental health crisis.

Sedentary activity leads to weight gain more like.

Nonetheless, the restrictions became a cause of stress and distress. I did every assessment they chucked my way, to show compliance. Their restricting me and not telling me why was plain cruel. I tried to convince the sergeant, who I thought was on my team, to let me come out in the car with them and find this person.

"I promise I will point out the window at the relevant spots to look at and check. If you're happy to do the checking bit, I will do the pointing bit, and I will stay locked in the car if I have to."

A bit like a prisoner might actually do when driving around pointing out other crimes, so they may all be taken into consideration coinciding with their arrested offence. *I can relate.*

I don't think this sergeant believed I would actually stay in the car. We will never know now. I was a woman of my word, though.

I had a good idea where this wanted on warrant and missing potentially suicidal person would be. I was sure of it. It would be an intelligence-led area search. Despite being two weeks later, the likelihood with some homeless souls is that they really don't move far in that time. They have habits and spots they frequent. Just like regular folk. Otherwise known as patches.

On the sergeant's job and their orders higher up the rank, received but not yet communicated with me, they weren't allowed to facilitate this cheeky, off the record area search to properly conclude that job from two weeks earlier. Control room kept closing the log report down, I kept requesting it be reopened until a point in time a satisfactory welfare check had been successfully conducted on the person. Who else was checking all the loose ends of a job were tied up? It was just me. Like it had been shown in the jobs involving drunk young men back in 2010.

Who the heck is this police constable (PC), who keeps

reopening this log? This no one. Control room staff had special powers over all policing matters.

There was now a wanted-on warrant to boot; so technically this would never be a simple welfare check. Although it would be a comprehensive one. Ask any officer, a wanted-on warrant arrest is both simple, quick and efficient to deal with. You do your arresting statement, handover in custody, and that's the job done and complete.

I'm not talking about the ones who go down kicking and screaming and need helicopters and full riot gear.

I was giving any officer not on mandatory restrictions an 'easy' job on a plate.

I even emailed my old neighbourhood team colleagues, as I knew of at least one of them who lived for those wanted on warrant arrests. There was a time when we had to submit returns so a wanted-on warrant ticked the arrests box nicely, making both constable and supervision look 'busy'.

The purpose of such returns, so far as I understood them, was so that come Monday morning, the senior management team could go over the previous week's activity. Tell stakeholders 'successes' in statistical form. But ten arrests doesn't mean ten qualitative arrests. It just means ten arrests. Not ten ending in court and convictions, etc. Data is as good as it is input.

Unfortunately, none of the old kin from neighbourhood or senior management team would reply to do the check for me either.

There was no one at times to call on.

Which was all the more disappointing to me. Someone was probably telling them not to assist me. As some of them I know would have if they could have.

As for this sergeant not wanting to let me get out in the car with them for a bit, unless it was to head to a team meal, I thought they had a strain of wayward like me in them, to be a bit naughty and break the rules sometimes when they needed bending somewhat. A lot. It was their spouse's cancer that got me thinking about that netball court overlooked by the cancer treatment block at a hospital. To be having cancer treatment, yet to be able to look from the windows to life going on and playing outside, could that instil more life? Or to those in rehabilitation, like my school peer had been in before finding amputee football. Netball, basketball, or any sport for that matter, could be any ability play. We'd find your way.

What the sergeant did say was this:

"If you happen to find them on your lunch break, that's a different matter."

"You got it, sarge. I'll see you later."

With the warrant paperwork all squared, police national computer (PNC) updated and ready to go... I hopped out the restricted office chair and tactically went feral for a bit.

I guess one theory is because they thought I was mad. How would I know where this random wandering and homeless vagrant might be? Maybe they thought I would get lost and use my time out of their way. Two weeks after the initial call. The fact is, I did and would know. Just no one ever listened to me. Because I was marked up under mental health and as a mad woman.

It was a bit of an extended half an hour break that time, but I didn't care. It was my last couple of days anyway. Neither did supervision. Get lost problem. Twenty minutes on the train later, I arrived. I found an individual's sleeping apparatus and there was someone underneath it. I took some discreet pictures and thought I am too early. I will come back later. Let them sleep. I became a tourist in my own jurisdiction. I walked around for a bit. Had an urgent need to poo, so used the public facilities nearby, then returned to the office. That time I paid my fifty pence to the system to drop off. My pick up, wasn't quite ready.

One thing I cannot understand is how we as humans are expected to leave our homes each day without recourse to public toilets the whole while. Where have they all gone?

I couldn't focus on much else but wanting to get back to the sleeping bag equipment to see who laid beneath it. It had to be them, right. Alive and well-ish. I would have to come back to this very spot later. It was proving a very long wait to get back there. On route back, I reminisced over some London landmarks – historical places where people had experienced worse treatment than I; like executions. Now that was unfair.

Back in the office now, on the broken chair, late turn shift coming in, the buzz of emails and computers being checked – and with four p.m. looming, I packed up and repeated the journey. Twenty minutes back I go again. Within a ten-minute walk from the initial locale originating call for service.

This time on top of the sleeping bag there was our person as broad as daylight. I knew them all right.

So I made the call:

"I have eyes on and need a unit to come pick us up. I am on restrictions, I am good, safe distance away – but I will deal if you would allow a vehicle to pick us up. PLEASE."

Silence.

Two hours later, the daylight was fading, my phone battery was dying, and it was starting to rain.

"Come home, love," my ex-husband told me. "Come home."

With that, I took a picture of 'you are here' on one of the London maps… and went home, depleted that no one from Met, BTP or City would come out. Nor were they likely to. Why? Was it because I had called them? Was it because it was a homeless, drug-addicted ex sex worker vagrant that no one wanted to deal with? Why? I wrote to the Home Secretary afterward; they didn't reply either. I, like them, didn't matter enough. No one would 'retweet' a no one. No one would miss a 'no one', would they?

There had been an unwritten rule in the police and that was always to look after the three Ps.

Prisoners.

Prostitutes.

And

Property.

Still, some wouldn't.

Prisoners and prostitutes would be better covered under People now, adding Places with Property would be my three Ps.

The following day, I submitted all the paperwork and intelligence (pictures of the sleeping gear and 'you are here' map) so they may be found again, probably in the same spot, later. If they hadn't upped and left it and jumped in front of the next train, that is.

As any problem with suicide is it's unpredictable. If you think and know someone to be having those thoughts, time is of the essence to get them under the care of a mental health professional – quick smart. I think the police got lucky in this case, this time. Two weeks later and no death occurred this time on their watch. But had it, there was a cluster fuck of multi-agency failures to contribute to that preventable death.

For two weeks, I evidenced what I did each day to bid an

intervention, should the worst occur, and I have to justify my role within the system. I may have well been tied and gagged to that broken chair. I didn't mind having my name all over jobs, where stakes were high and where I knew I had purpose to drive towards their resolution.

I then took anything personal from the office with me and left for good. I was happy to wrap up on that job. It was over to them, or anyone else who had energy left to care. I had some faith still left in our safeguarding team at least, who were the last people I contacted about whipping some action into shape. If they could.

I applied to go back into safeguarding part time afterward. For some reason, I didn't get through the application sift.

Then I was done.

Policing done.

I was going home to be surrounded with love, to go forward, and surround myself only with those who want to be around me now. Those that, if I called them, would come. I don't need to fight for my place where I know I am not welcome or wanted any longer.

What went well:
   Got a new job.

That didn't go so well:
   Grieved the old one.

Finale

When it comes to telling your story, perhaps it is a blog piece you could start with. It only needs an audience of one, at the end of the day – you. The free website tool I used was called WordPress. If you are proud of it, stand by it, and own it, it's good enough. In telling and sharing your story, you just never know who in turn it could go on to help. As many people land at crossroad points in their life, I know how despairing it can be to land there with no meaningful support left to aide you.

Whether it was the police or my mental ill health, or a combination that saw me alienated from society in a lot of ways, it was one of the reasons I had felt so alone, at the verge of suicide. The 'what is the point'. Getting a dog saved me.

Much of my intention to leave the police was that, at the crossroads, you can always turn back. You can always go back to the comfort of what you know and love. It's why people go back to abusive relationships, right?

You can always stay put. Not test the boundaries and borders. But from what I have experienced, with the unexpected turn of events such as Covid-19 and a world pandemic, I have thrived and lived through, all whilst outside restrictive relationships. For me, the police and as a tube driver instead.

Only recently, whilst stationary at one of the tube stations, I spotted a colleague who I had previously worked with. They had made both racist and sexist slurs during my time spent with them in the police van in their company. Them driving, of course. Me, the passenger. Now here they were, operating in 'plain clothes', I knew to target the people they showed hate towards. So called 'pick pockets'. Now a lawful authority given to them to target the group they hated. Yet, there they were, the same place, same time, almost as I had been with them five years prior. Same job. Same pay. Yet here I was, moved on – and not staying still. The hate they shared stopped only their own progression. Any time I reported racism or any matter within the ranks, nothing changed for that individual, like it did for me. The phrase "You stay there, I'll fuck off" rings clear.

What rings true of this is those who get stuck on their previous history or story; the best advice I have got for this is, "You could be overlooking the next opportunity by being stuck in the past." Wise words said by a Harley Therapist at Harleytherapy.com.

Now much of my happiness and focus lies mostly not whilst at work, but outside of it. In reality, those 'could turn back' reassurances more often than not turn out to be, in reality, life's little efforts in keeping the surprises coming when you least expect them. The next opportunity could be missed by dwelling so strongly on the past.

You have to keep open to opportunities occurring for you in the future. Be in the present and find space to start all over again if needs be.

Suicide is a final act, of which all further opportunities become extinguished to you thereafter. As long as you have air in your lungs and your heart is beating, you'll be OK.

It's OK.

If you need to hear it, read it, or see it – just don't do it. People want you to stay. Firstly, and secondly, anyone who doesn't care about how they have treated you in this life isn't going to care any more on your demise, if anything – they will care even less. I thank you for your existence.

Religious or not, I can say with some clarity that I am not sure what demon I upset in doing my suicidal-ish acts previously. But for a little short time afterward, I got plagued with 'knocks' or 'bangs', as if I had tip toed close to the edge of something I should not have done.

Whatever you believe, I now hold a value that, if I was to kill myself, I would be reincarnated into a life more difficult than this one – and this one, after all, hasn't and isn't so bad. I don't want to try out any afterlife yet anyway.

Whether you believe in poltergeists or not, I don't believe I imagined the events that followed ever so briefly afterward.

A knock on a first-floor window wasn't my first and last stalkerish ex-boyfriend again.

I totally appreciate how mad this all must sound. I do accept I may have been incredibly unwell and in a dream-like state also, as a rationalist and scientist. Religion is important to me too.

Keep an open mind, they say. As for ghosts, then, I think they soon depart again on seeing my baseline is that of an actually fairly happy and optimistic person. Sorry to disappoint.

Depression isn't all sadness.

Future return?

I wouldn't rule it completely out, but I don't think they would have me, unless someone from the Crown intervened. Having written to the Home Secretary and got no reply, there isn't anywhere else to go to. The Crown could hold oversight to outlive any swift turn in government. My "What about the Crown"? got a laugh from the university lecturers, but I was serious in my question. The Professor, came to life, answered albeit briefly, that I perhaps was expecting too much from The Crown. The Crown whom, if the end of the world did arrive, would blast off into space, on a specially designed rocket, with a sign at its rear end "General election now", or so I would imagine No. 10 Downing Street staff reading it.

As for now, I'll 'serve' in the best way I know how to, working as a tube driver. It is at least front-row of a roller coaster ride. That'll do me.

I'm underground now. Yet flying high.

Maybe see you around.